Willard W. Glazier

The Capture, the Prison Pen, and the Escape, Giving an Account of Prison Life in the South

Willard W. Glazier

The Capture, the Prison Pen, and the Escape, Giving an Account of Prison Life in the South

ISBN/EAN: 9783744747752

Printed in Europe, USA, Canada, Australia, Japan

Cover: Foto ©ninafisch / pixelio.de

More available books at **www.hansebooks.com**

THE CAPTURE,

THE

Prison Pen and the Escape,

GIVING AN

ACCOUNT OF PRISON LIFE IN THE SOUTH,

PRINCIPALLY AT

RICHMOND, DANVILLE, MACON, SAVANNAH, CHARLESTON, COLUMBIA, MILLIN, SALISBURY AND ANDERSONVILLE: DESCRIBING THE ARRIVAL OF PRISONERS, PLANS OF ESCAPE, WITH INCIDENTS AND ANECDOTES OF PRISON LIFE;

EMBRACING, ALSO,

THE ADVENTURES OF AN ESCAPE FROM COLUMBIA, S. C., RECAPTURE, TRIAL AS SPY, AND FINAL ESCAPE FROM SYLVANIA, GEORGIA.

With Illustrations.

By WILLARD W. GLAZIER,

LATE LIEUTENANT, HARRIS LIGHT CAVALRY.

"We speak that we do know, and testify that we have seen.

ALBANY:
J. MUNSELL, 82 STATE STREET.
1866.

TO THE
WIDOWS, CHILDREN, FATHERS, MOTHERS, BROTHERS,
SISTERS, FRIENDS, AND SURVIVING COMRADES

Of the Thousands of Brave Men

Who left the Pleasures and Comforts of Home,
Abandoned cherished Enterprises
and business Schemes

FOR THE PURPOSE OF SERVING THEIR COUNTRY,

And who have been Captured by the Enemy
while in the faithful performance
of their Duty,

AND GONE DOWN

To untimely Graves through unparalleled Sufferings,
Is this Volume most Respectfully

DEDICATED

BY   THE AUTHOR.

"Hallow ye each unmarked grave,
　Make their memory sure and blest;
For their lives they nobly gave
　And their spirits are at rest."

PREFACE.

The following pages are offered to inquiring minds with the hope that they may throw some light upon the inhuman treatment we received in southern prisons.

They do not pretend to give a complete history of prison life in the south — only a part. Others are contributing sketches for the dark picture, which at the best, can but poorly illustrate the fearful atrocities of our brutal keepers.

For the want of much information on this subject, it is impossible for me to give an exact account of the number of deaths in southern prisons. Still, if we consider the statements of several who have reduced their calculations to figures, we may arrive at a more correct conclusion than we otherwise should. Robert H. Kellogg, Sergeant Maj., 16th Conn. Volunteers, who was at Andersonville and Florence, says the deaths at the latter place were 12 per cent per month. Mr. Richardson, correspondent of the *New York Tribune*, says it was 13 per cent at Salisbury for the same time. There were 13,000 deaths at Andersonville. Mr. Kellogg affirms that one-half of his regiment died in about seven months. Let us suppose that the prisoners will average 25,000 from January 1, 1862, to January 1, 1865, and the deaths to be nine per cent per month, or 2,250; then multiply by 36 months, and we have 81,000 deaths. Had we been provided with such clothing, shelter and food as the laws of health absolutely require, it is probable that there would not have been more than one-eighth of the actual number of deaths. Hence, we conclude that 70,875 have fallen victims to inhuman treatment. My figures with regard to the number of prisoners and the percentage of deaths may be too large; but allowing that my estimates are nearly right, the awful carnage of the battle-field has not exceeded the frightful mortality of the prison pen. Whether the rebels have intentionally murdered our unfortunate soldiers or not, I leave the reader to decide.

It was not the intention to publish my experience until several weeks after my escape. I kept a diary and journal from the time of my capture. Upon reading portions of it to some of my friends, they persuaded me to amplify, and put it in a readable form.

The rough manuscript was, for the most part, prepared in a brush shanty at Columbia; sitting on the ground, and writing upon the back of an old tin plate. Capt. Kelly, 1st Kentucky Cavalry, brought a part of that manuscript through the lines by concealing it in an old regulation hat, which he wore during his escape. I smuggled the remainder through in the lining of my jacket.

The Appendix is principally the work of Robert J. Fisher, late captain 17th Missouri Volunteers, being taken from his lithograph, entitled the "Libby Prison Memorial." To these, as well as those friends who have expressed an interest in the work, and in various ways aided in promoting it, my sincere thanks are tendered.

WILLARD W. GLAZIER

Albany, N. Y., Nov 12, 1865.

CONTENTS.

	PAGE.
Preface,	5
List of Illustrations,	25
The Principal Rebel Prisons, and Where they were Located,	27
Introduction,	29

CHAPTER I.

Enlistment and Term of Service,	35
Organization of the Harris Light Cavalry,	36
Term of Service,	36

CHAPTER II.

The Capture,	37
Cavalry Fight at New Baltimore,	37
Gen Stuart Orders a Charge,	38
March to Culpepper,	38
Our Sufferings on the Way,	39
The Former Residence of Capt. Semmes,	39
Robbing Prisoners,	39

CONTENTS.

	PAGE.
Gen. Lee in Full Retreat for the Rapidan,	39
Dialogue with a Rebel,	40

CHAPTER III.

Libby Prison,	41
Arrival at Richmond,	41
Manner in which we were treated by the Rebel Officers on arriving at Libby Prison,	42
Our Reception by the Prisoners,	42
Maj. Turner's Office,	42
Description of Libby Prison,	45
Character of Major Turner,	46
Sickness in the Hospital,	48
Prisoner Shot by a Sentinel,	46
Encouraging Prospects of the Prisoners,	48
My Removal to Libby Prison Hospital,	49
Plan of Escape,	52
Rumored Exchange of Surgeons,	52
Exchange of Surgeons,	54
Thanksgiving Day in Libby Prison,	55
Our Manner of Correspondence—The Rebels discover the Secret,	57
Hypocrisy of the Rebels,	55
Issue of Private Boxes,	56
Detention of a Love Letter,	58
Mortality on Belle Island,	59
Rebel Method of Burying Our Dead,	59
Death of My Sister Elvira,	60

CONTENTS.

	PAGE.
Sad News from Home,	60
Gen. Bragg's Defeat,	60
Suffering from Cold,	62
Distribution of Clothing among the Prisoners,	63
Gen. Meade Retires Toward Fredericksburg,	63
The Manner in which we Amuse Ourselves,	64
An Escape and its Consequences,	65
My Return from the Hospital,	65
Exchange Rumors,	66
Barbarous Treatment of the Sick,	66
The New Year in Libby,	68
Preparations for a Dance,	68
List of Rations Issued to Us,	69
Punishment for Singing our National Songs,	69
Tunneling,	70
One Hundred and Fifty Prisoners Missing,	70
Maj. Turner Allows an Issue of Boxes,	71
Capture of Escaped Prisoners,	71
The Great Tunnel,	72
The Plan of Operation,	73
Conveniences for Performing the Work,	73
Each Man Determined to be First Out,	74
Escape of Prisoners,	75
The Roll Call,	75
Lateush Discovers the Tunnel,	76
The Guard in Castle Thunder,	76
Kilpatrick's Raid,	76
Our Organization,	77

CONTENTS.

	PAGE.
Negro Guide Shot for Perfidy,	78
Gen. Kilpatrick's Designs Thwarted,	78
Death of Col. Dahlgren,	79
Rebel Mode of Treating Raiders,	79
Method of Communicating with the Raiders,	80
The Prison Undermined,	81
Share Our Rations with the Raiders,	81
The Special Exchange,	82
"Exchange on the Brain,"	82
Nearly Detected in Assisting the Raiders,	83
Amusement at the Expense of the "Fresh Fish,"	84
Prisoners from Plymouth,	84
Refuse to Give us Wood,	87
"Corn Dodgers,"	88
Gen. Lee Reported to be Defeated,	88
Farewell to Libby,	89

CHAPTER IV.

Arrived at Danville, Virginia,	90
Escape from the Cars,	90
New Plans for Escape,	91
C. S. Military Prison, Danville, Va.,	92
Our Rations at Danville Prison	92
Sleeping Spoon Fashion,	93
"Uncle Bob" Comes off Second Best,	94
A Large Tunnel in Process of Digging,	94
In Cattle Cars, near Greensboro', N. C.,	95
The Rebels Alarmed,	96

CONTENTS.

	PAGE.
Conscripts for Lee's Army,	96
An Attempt to Escape,	97
Near Charlotte, N. C.,	97
Prisoners Attempt to Escape by Burying Themselves in the Ground,	98
We Entertain Citizens,	98
Plans for Escape,	98
Columbia, South Carolina,	99
Augusta, Georgia,	100

CHAPTER V.

At Macon, Georgia, Camp Oglethorpe,	102
Macon, its Military Importance,	102
Maj. Turner at Macon,	103
The Dead Line,	103
New Arrivals,	104
Firing upon a Prisoner,	104
Our Rations,	105
Notice from the Rebel Authorities,	106
Our Method of Digging Tunnels,	106
Our Tunnel Discovered,	110
Unpleasant Consequences,	110
Our Appeal to Capt. Gibbs,	111
Murder of Lieut. Grierson,	111
Rebel Favors,	112
A Meeting held in Accordance with Rebel Suggestions,	113
New Tunnels,	114

CONTENTS.

	PAGE.
Our Plans for Escape Frustrated,	114
Sentinels are Instructed to Shoot down Prisoners,	115
Special Order No. 9,	115
Scurvy,	116
Afflicted with the Scurvy,	116
Fourth of July—Our Celebration,	117
Col. Thorpe Makes a Speech,	119
Capt. Gibbs Orders us to Disperse,	119
Special Orders No. 6,	120
"Skirmishing,"	120
The Author sells his Buttons to save Life,	122
Removal of Prisoners,	123
A General Exchange of Prisoners Anticipated,	123

CHAPTER VI.

At Savannah, Georgia, Camp Davidson,	126
Preparations for Defence of Macon,	126
Description of Savannah,	127
Kind Treatment at Savannah,	128
A Comparison of Rebel Prisons,	129
Better Rations,	130
Prisoners Attempt to Escape,	130
Brick Ovens,	131
Tunneling,	132
Our Scheme Exposed by a Cow,	132
Joy Without, Death Within the Stockade,	133
Nothing but a Damned Yankee,	134
Death of Capt. McGinnis,	134

CONTENTS. 15

	PAGE.
Inhumanity of Col. Wayne,	134
Exchange of Army Chaplains and Surgeons,	135
Kindness of Ladies,	135
Heavy Cannonading in the Direction of Charleston,	136
Rumored Removal to Charleston,	137

CHAPTER VII.

In Charleston Jail Yard,	138
One of our Men fired upon by the Guard,	139
The Burnt District,	141
Charleston Jail and its Inmates,	143
A Friend,	144
Inclined to be Distrustful,	144
An Act of true Nobleness,	144
Genuine Patriotism,	145
A higher Language than the Written,	146
The last Visit,	147
An Original Song,	148
Andersonville,	149
The Ground a Mass of Lice,	149
Awful Condition of the Hospital,	150
Great Suffering,	150
Living Death,	151
A Thunder Storm,	152
Refused Admission to the Jail,	152
A Contrast,	153
Shells a Subject of Discussion,	154
Roper Hospital,	157

16 CONTENTS

	PAGE.
Sisters of Charity,	158
Yellow Fever,	160

CHAPTER VIII.

Removal to Columbia, Camp Sorghum,	162
Treated Kindly by the 32d Ga.,	162
Rebel Vigilance,	163
Peace Movements,	163
Columbia,	164
Morning after the Storm,	168
Turned out to Grass,	168
News from the Army,	170
Distribution of Clothing,	170
A Day of Joy,	170
Voting upon the Presidential Candidates,	171
The Test and its Result,	172
An Escape,	174
Rejoicing Over a Successful Escape,	175
A Prisoner Shot,	176
Thoughts of Home,	177
Allowed to get Wood by Taking a Parole,	179
My Old Shoes,	181
Turning Night into Day,	182
A Day of Anxiety,	182
Deception Practiced by the Prison Authorities,	183
Lieut. Parker Fearfully Mangled by Dogs,	184
Caught by Hounds,	184
Issuing Meat Rations at Camp Sorghum,	187

CONTENTS.

	PAGE.
Governor Brown's Proclamation,	189
Heavy Frosts—No Blankets,	190
Sleeping in the Middle,	190
No Prospect of an Exchange,	191
Renewed Determination to Escape,	191

CHAPTER IX.

The Escape from Columbia,	193
Out on Parole,	193
Passing the Dead Line,	194
Meeting Negroes,	195
Blind Roads,	196
A Picket of Eight Men,	196
"I Dun No What Make Dem Niggers Run So,"	197
Another Picket,	197
The Escape—Searching for the Road at Night,	199
Kindness of Mrs. Taylor,	201
A Royal Breakfast,	202
Met a Negro,	203
A Prayer Meeting,	203
A Negro Guide,	204
The "Augusta Constitutionalist,"	205
Crossing the North Edisto,	205
The Road terminates in a Swamp,	206
Other Difficulties,	207
My Companion's Misfortune,	208
Pursued by Bushwhackers,	209
Meeting Escaped Prisoners,	210

CONTENTS.

	PAGE.
Approaching a Negro,	210
An Attempt to Travel by Rail,	211
Good Music — Greatly Encouraged,	212
Followed by a Hound,	212
A Happy Mistake,	213
A Race,	214
Something for the Haversack,	214
Traveling with a Guide,	215
In a Cypress Swamp on the Savannah,	216
Viewing our little Craft by Moonlight,	216
Crossing the Savannah in a Cypress Tree Canoe,	217
Bailing for Life,	217
Alligators,	218
The North Star,	218
Cavalry Patrol,	219
My Old Shoes,	219
Fording Streams and Backing Each Other,	222
Chased by Hounds,	223
Acting the Part of a Rebel,	224
"De Planter Was a Bushwhacker,"	227
A Confederate Officer,	228
My Horse Shot at Waynesboro,	228
Transferred,	228
Our Clothing Excites Suspicion,	229
Determined to Have a Breakfast,	230
"Mr. Brown's,"	230
Accidentally Seen by a Planter,	231
A Critical Situation,	232

CONTENTS.

	PAGE.
Pursued by Hounds,	232
Duping Rebel Couriers,	233

CHAPTER X.

Re-captured by a Rebel Picket,	234
The Challenge,	236
Acting as Scout to Gen. Hardie,	236
Regarded as a Yankee Spy,	238
A Kind Act,	240
An Attempt to Bribe the Guard,	241
"Let 'Em Stretch Hemp,"	242
Apparently Unable to Walk,	243
Once More in the Saddle,	243
The Escape and Pursuit,	244
Arrival at Wheeler's Head Quarters,	246
Two Live Yanks in the Jail Yard,	249
Method of Accounting for Absentees,	252
Good News,	255
A Favor,	255

CHAPTER XI.

The Escape from Sylvania, Ga.,	256
Lieut. J. W. Wright, 10th Iowa Volunteers,	256
The Plan for Escape,	256
"Escape on the Brain,"	257
Escaping with Rations Intended for the Rebel Guard,	258
Old Richard,	260

	PAGE.
Confiding our Plans to a Negro,	261
Concealed in an Old Pine Tree Top,	262
In a Swamp near Springfield, Ga.,	263
Rebel Deserters,	265
Renewed Obstacles,	266
A Proposition,	266
The Interview with Mrs. Keyton — Turning the Tables,	267
Ill Fated Dixie,	273
Gen. Sherman Just Where They Wanted Him,	273
Startled by the Yelping of Hounds,	275
Bushwhackers in Pursuit,	275
A Narrow Escape,	276
An Amusing Incident,	278
Rebel Scouts,	280
Efforts to Obtain a Guide,	281
Colored Man No. 3,	281
March Dasher,	282
"I'll Do It, Massa, If God Be My Helper,"	282
Uneasy Until Prayer Was Offered for Our Benefit,	282
The Negro's Clock Needs No Repairing,	283
"Gemmen, Now Ize Ready,"	283
A Group of Blue Coats,	284
Maj. Turner was not There,	284

CHAPTER XII.

Arrival at Savannah,	286
Regarded as Spies,	287

CONTENTS.

	PAGE.
Pronounced Genuine Union Soldiers,	288
Christmas Dinner,	288
At Kilpatrick's Head Quarters,	289
On Board the Steamship Planter,	290
On Board the Ashland,	291
In a Gale off Cape Hatteras,	291
Arrival at New York,	292

CHAPTER XIII.

At Millin,	294
Camp Lawton,	294
Testimony of Sergt. W. Goodyear,	294
The Inclosure,	295
Average Number of Deaths per Day,	596
Daily Allowance of Rations,	297
Voting at Millin Prison,	298
Inducements to Enter the Rebel Service,	298
Came too Near the Dead Line,	301
Testimony of O. R. Dahl,	301
Murder of Lieut. Turbayne,	301

CHAPTER XIV.

Salisbury Penitentiary,	303
Testimony of Messrs. Richardson and Brown,	303
Great Suffering for Want of Bread and Shelter,	304
"Give Them Quarter Rations,"	305
Terrible Condition of the Hospitals,	306

Meeting Among the Prisoners, ... 306
Mr. Brown's Description of Salisbury Prison,..... 308

CHAPTER XV.

At Andersonville, ... 311
Testimony of Ira E. Forbes, ... 311
Capture and Removal to Camp Sumter, ... 312
At Tarboro, ... 312
Traffic with the Rebels, ... 313
Cattle Cars Styled "Carriages" by Rebels, ... 314
Generosity of the Citizens of Charleston, ... 315
Arrival at Andersonville, ... 316
Capt. Wirz, the Little Foreigner, ... 316
Suffering at Andersonville, ... 317
The Dead Line, ... 318
A Prisoner Shot, ... 319
Burial of the Dead, ... 320
A Prisoner Shot, ... 320
Intense Mental Trials, ... 322
Removal of Prisoners from Andersonville, ... 323
Scurvy, ... 324
Rations Issued by the United States Government to Rebel Prisoners of War, ... 325
Statement of Clothing Issued to Prisoners of War at Fort Delaware, ... 326
Union Prisoners from Dixie's Sunny Land, ... 327

CONTENTS.

APPENDIX,

PAGE.

Containing the Name, Rank and Regiment of the Officers who were imprisoned at Richmond, Danville, Macon, Savannah, Charleston, Columbia, Charlotte, Raleigh and Goldsborough, 1864 and 1865,... 331

LIST OF ILLUSTRATIONS.

1. Rebel Mode of Capturing Escaped Prisoners, Frontispiece.

   PAGE.
2. View of Libby Prison,............................... 43
3. Interior View of Libby Prison,..................... 85
4. Tunneling (The Narrow Path to Freedom),..... 107
5. Issuing Meat Rations at Camp Sorghum,......... 185
6. The Escape — Searching for the Road at Night, 199
7. Came too near the Dead Line, ... 299

THE PRINCIPAL REBEL PRISONS, AND WHERE THEY WERE LOCATED.

Libby, Richmond, Va.
Danville, Pottsylvania county, Va.
Macon, Ga., known south as Camp Oglethorpe.
Savannah, Ga., known south as Camp Davidson.
Charleston, S. C.
Columbia, S. C., known south as Camp Sorghum.
Andersonville, Sumter county, Ga., known south as Camp Sumter.
Millin, Burke Co., Ga., known south as Camp Lawton.
Florence, Darlington county, S. C.
Salisbury, Rowan county, N. C.
Tyler, Smith county, Texas.
Cahaba, Dallas county, Alabama.
Castle Thunder, Richmond, Va.
Belle Isle, in James river, near Richmond.
Blackstone, S. C.
Raleigh, N. C.

INTRODUCTION.

In presenting this little volume to the public, let us bespeak for it the welcome due to truth, wherever found. It is not pretentious. The author is a young man and a patriot.

He comes with no high sounding claims—no grand display of literary wealth; simply as a fellow being—a man who has suffered and fought for his country. A returned soldier, escaped from the horrors of southern prisons, he appeals to our feelings of humanity and our gratitude. He bears his honest wounds, and lifts his manly voice in testimony of the guilt of the merciless leaders of the great rebellion. Additional proofs he offers of the atrocities the slave power has practiced upon our poor boys who meekly and heroically endured sufferings, privations and indignities to which all history furnishes no parallel, and which only trained and depraved miscreants could inflict.

As we follow him from his peaceful home among the pleasant valleys of the St. Lawrence, where no clank of chains was ever heard—no moan of starvation ever saddened the free air—where the odious emblem of traitors and tyrants was never unfurled—we become identified with him in all his wanderings, dangers, and escapes, and, borne on the irresistible tide of sympathy, we almost feel his pain, and weep with him in misfortune.

There are passages of great beauty and exceeding, nay, painful interest in this book of our young countryman. Indeed, many pages would be worthy of our best writers.

Sentiments of lofty patriotism, heroic fortitude, moral and spiritual purity, constantly win our admiration and endear him to our hearts.

He has not fallen into the egotism, so difficult to avoid in a work of this kind. His modesty is only equaled by a spirit of self-sacrifice, a love of liberty and country. He speaks in bitter rebuke of the Confederate government, of slavery and its degraded minions.

Often, did we not know from others, and from his unquestioned integrity, the truth of what he relates, we should doubt the awful realities he pictures; saying, in this age, in this land of freedom, such things could never be.

And now the question arises—how can we account for the barbarism of the southern leaders, and their debased turnkeys and hirelings? They are of our blood, were born in a Christian land, and in the nineteenth century. How does it happen that they have been guilty of crimes and ferocity that the tawny savage of the Pacific slope would blush to perpetrate? Alas, there can be but one reply: born and bred to tyranny and vice; nurtured in shameful debauchery; ashamed of honest labor; accustomed to appropriate the fruit of another's toil; to employ brute force to trample on the rights of others. Educated to practices a northern *man* would shudder to contemplate, they have stained with blood and horror the records of their unholy rebellion, and steeped in shame the name of Southern Chivalry. Their vaunted superiority and haughty claims to the title of gentlemen, have become a by-word and a jeer.

We should pity them, if we could forget to abhor. As it is—with the fearful monuments of Belle Isle, Libby, Columbia, Salisbury, Andersonville, and others before our eyes—with the living victims of their depravity among us—with the groans of our murdered soldiers in every cemetery—with our lunatic asylums, tenanted by their wretched captives, driven to madness by slow starvation, exposure and hardened cruelty, can we say of Jefferson Davis, his generals and agents, go; enjoy the blessings of sun and air, health and liberty? Shall the earth fester beneath the tread of monsters more dangerous and terrible than the deadly boa or ferocious tiger.

Let the avenging justice of the righteous Father of all be our answer.

He who has led us through this Red Sea of our brother's blood, to the green hills and sunny plains of Peace and Freedom, He will reveal himself in the future of our country, to bless her if deserving—to punish if she forgets her duty to her slaughtered sons—her trampled bondsmen—her soldiers, their widows and orphans.

>"Think not the Eternal's ear is deaf,
>   His sleepless vision dim;
> Think, ye, the soul's blood may not rise
>   From that far land to Him?"

With a cordial endorsement of the book before us, chiefly for its entire simplicity and truthfulness, we commend it to all loyal souls.

HELEN RICH.

Canton, St. Lawrence Co., N. Y., Oct. 1, 1865.

THE CAPTURE,

THE Prison Pen and the Escape.

CHAPTER I.

ENLISTMENT AND TERM OF SERVICE.

In listening to an adventure, personal or otherwise, the hearer very naturally desires to know who is addressing him. Therefore, kind reader, know that I was born in the town of Fowler, St. Lawrence Co., N. Y., August 22d, 1841.

I enlisted as a private in the company raised by Clarence Buel, for the 2d Regiment of N. Y. Cavalry (Harris Light), Aug. 6th, 1861, at Troy, N. Y. I will not enter upon any elaborate description of the emotions or motives which led me to enter the service, my reasons will be easily conjectured by all loyal hearts. The Harris Light Cavalry was organized by J. Mansfield Davies of New York, as colonel, and Judson Kilpatrick of New Jersey, as lieutenant colonel. The regiment was composed of men from New York, New Jersey, Connecticut, Vermont, Pennsylvania and Indiana. It was originally intended for the regular army, and was known for some time as the 7th U. S. Cavalry; but the Regular Cavalry being reduced to six regiments, we were assigned to New York, as she had contributed the largest number of men to the organization. We were ordered to Washington during the latter part of August, and after a month's drill, crossed the Potomac, and encamped in front of the enemy at Munson's Hill. From this time until my capture at the close of the campaign in '63, I served with my regiment, which shared the varied fortunes of the Army of the Potomac, under its successive commanders, McClellan, McDowell, Pope, Burnside, Hooker and Meade, but in the more immediate commands of Bayard, Stoneman, Pleasonton, Gregg and Kilpatrick.

CHAPTER II.

THE CAPTURE.

In the cavalry fight at New Baltimore, Va., Oct. 19th, 1863, Gen. Kilpatrick with his small division (which had been greatly reduced by the fearful losses of the summer campaign), was opposed to Stuart's entire command. Kilpatrick, who was acting upon the offensive, had thrown his force across Broad Run, at Buckland, when, to our surprise, we were attacked in rear by Fitz Hugh Lee, which was the signal for Stuart to commence the attack in front and General Gordon on the flanks. In this emergency General Kilpatrick, with that coolness and decision which has ever characterized him as a great leader of cavalry, ordered his whole force to wheel about and charge the columns of Lee. The "Harris Light," having been in front while advancing, now became the rear guard, and by this movement we were compelled to meet the desperate charges of the enemy in pursuit; having reached a little rise of ground we made a stand and for some time checked the advance of the rebels by pouring into their ranks deadly volleys from our carbines and revolvers. General Stuart, who was at the head of his command, saw clearly that he could only dislodge us by a charge, and ordering it lead his men in person. Our men stood firm and were soon engaged in a hand to hand conflict with the advancing columns of the foe.

At this juncture my horse was shot under me, and our little party, outnumbered ten to one, was hurled back by the overpowering force of the rebels, their whole command riding over myself and horse. Being severely injured by the fall of my horse and by the charging squadrons that passed over me, I was insensible for several moments, and when I became conscious of my situation found that I was being carried rapidly from the scene of action under a *rebel* guard. My arms had been stripped from me, my pockets rifled, and watch taken. Once a prisoner, I was hurried from the field to Warrenton jail, and from thence to Culpepper, Orange Court House, Gordonsville and Richmond. I shall never forget our march from Warrenton to Culpepper; it was one of the severest tramps of my life. We started at sunrise and went by way of Sulphur Springs, which before the war was a stirring little town as well as a favorite summer resort for the F. F. V's of that vicinity, but is now in a ruinous condition, noted only as the former home of Capt. Semmes, commander of the pirate Alabama. The weather was exceedingly hot and the distance not less than thirty miles. Our guard was mounted and evinced but little sympathy for our unfortunate condition, as we endeavored to keep pace with them. Their great haste was owing to the fact that General Lee had been defeated at the battle of Bristoe, and was in full retreat for the Rapidan, our army in pursuit. None save those who have been in the cavalry service know how to sympathize with a dismounted cavalier if compelled to march on foot. Our sufferings were indescribable; curses and threats long and loud were freely indulged in by the guard because we could not walk faster. Six of our number fell by the wayside before we reached Culpepper from utter exhaustion. While at Warrenton most of our number were robbed of their clothing, watches, and in fact every thing which could excite either the curiosity or avarice of a rebel. One of these "chivalrous gentlemen" demanded my hat, over-coat and boots, when the following dialogue ensued:

Fed. The articles you demand are my personal property, and it is wrong for you to compel me to give them up.

Reb. We have authority from General Stuart to take from prisoners whatever we want.

Fed. I doubt your authority, sir, and if you are a gentleman you will not be guilty of stripping a defenceless prisoner.

Reb. I will show you my authority, you damned Yankee (drawing his pistol); now take off that coat or I will blow your brains out.

Fed. Blow away then, it is as well to be without brains as without clothing at this season of the year.

Johnny Reb was not quite disposed to fire upon me, and giving his head a shake rode off, thinking, no doubt, that he could supply his wants in another direction without wasting his ammunition.

CHAPTER III.

LIBBY PRISON.

October 23, 1863. We entered Richmond at an early hour in the morning, and were marched very hurriedly through town to this prison. While passing through the city we were subjected to the slang and insults of the citizens, who used every endeavor to impose upon us. One greeted us with "how *are you*, Blue Bellies?" "Why did'nt you all come into Richmond with your arms on?" Another sang out, "Hello Yanks, what do you think of Libby's?" Mrs. Secession remarked, "If they are the officers of the Yankee army, what must the privates be?" A chivalrous madam exclaimed, "O what a pity it is that our noble sons must be murdered by such miserable vagabonds!" We did not deign to notice their questions or remarks, but passed on in column of fours, keeping step, and with an air of perfect unconcern for the jesting which came from all sides. Arriving at the prison, we were first taken to Major Turner's office, where we were told that we must turn over all the gold and greenbacks in our possession. Our diaries were demanded, also the photographs and ambrotypes of our relatives and friends. After this most disgraceful robbery was concluded we were taken to the rooms occupied by the prisoners, and, as we met them, were amazed at their cries of "Fresh Fish." "Close up." "Where were you captured?" "What army do you belong to?" "Give him air," etc., etc. They did not abate their zeal in the use of the above expressions until several moments after our entrance. I soon learned that it was the universal custom to treat all new comers in the same manner.

I find the following officers of my regiment confined here: Maj. Samuel McIrvin, who was captured in the cavalry fight at Liberty Ford, while gallantly leading his battalion against the rebel Gen. Baker's brigade; Capt. Chas. Hasty, and Adj't P. O. Jones, also taken at Liberty Ford; Capt. H. H. Mason, captured on the Rappahannock; Quartermaster B. Coles, and Lieut. William Nyce, at Thoroughfare Gap; Lieut. J. A. Richardson, at Emmetsburg, Maryland; Lieut. Geo. H. Houston, Hazel river, Va., and

Libby Prison.

Lieut. A. C. Shaeffer, at Culpepper. They were all glad of the opportunity to hear from our armies, but deeply regretted that it was my misfortune to meet them in this awful place.

Libby Prison is an old and somewhat dilapidated building, belonging to the estate of John Enders. Before the war it was used by Libby and Son as a store house; but now it is used by southern fiends—for I cannot countenance a milder term—as a den of torture for such as may be so unfortunate as to fall into their hands. There are but few windows, and these small and carefully secured by iron grates. The sentinels are stationed in front of the windows, outside of the building, with orders to fire upon the first man who attempts to look out. We are here huddled together like sheep in a slaughter-house, awaiting the approach of those monsters, eager to destroy us by any mode of torture. The rooms are filthy and unfurnished. There are no chairs or bunks, and but few have blankets. They do not even furnish us with a necessary allowance of wood. We receive nothing but our rations; a meager allowance I can assure you. Yes, we do receive something else, viz., execrations and curses without measure. Previous to our becoming the occupants of this *Tartarian abode,* the sentinel in front of one of the windows fired at a prisoner confined in the room now occupied by us, the one for whom the shot was intended observing the motions of the guard, instantly dodged and thus escaped unharmed. But the ball, passing through and into the room above, there selected its unconscious victim, and without a moment's warning, launched him forth, prepared or otherwise, to appear before that God who knows every thought and purpose of the hearts of men. The commandant of the prison is Major Thomas P. Turner, of the C. S. A. He was formerly a student at West Point; but it is generally understood among the prisoners that he was expelled from that school for forgery. He was subsequently made captain in the rebel service, and, for efficiency as a great Yankee destroyer, has recently been promoted to the rank of major. We come in contact with Major Turner more than with any other of the prison authorities. He is a man whose character may easily be gathered from his countenance; for the hoof prints of appetite have made a lasting impression there. The utter depravity of the man seems to have gained a full and complete expression in every lineament of his countenance. To one who looks at the character and capacity of man, there is something inconceivably awful in its perversions. Look at it, if you can, as it comes fresh and plastic from its Maker; look at it as it stands before the world, stained and hardened. Conceive of a living soul, with the germs of faculties, which infinity cannot exhaust, and then follow it in its dark passage through life, as it stifles and kills, one by one, every inspiration and aspiration of its being until it becomes but a dead soul entombed in a living frame. Maimed and disfigured by the soul's pollution and war with right, its humanity becomes extinguished in the mad tyranny of animal ferocity. Such, I conclude, is the character of the man in question. It seems as though he has no feelings of humanity. He is, in fact, prepared for any crime that could enlist the evil passions of our nature. He uses every means at his command for annoying the prisoners. So atrocious are his deeds that the stings of conscience give him no rest day or night. He fancies that the prisoners are plotting to take his life, and has changed his quarters from the prison to a building across the street.

Oct. 29. There is at present much sickness in

the hospital. A large number of the prisoners captured during the fall campaign are suffering most severely from their wounds. As the rebels are utterly regardless of the sufferings of those under their charge, here the spirit of vengeance and brute ferocity is manifested in its most malignant form. The treatment that our officers, wounded and sick, receive at the hands of the Southern Chivalry is most brutal. It would chill the blood of him not entirely bereft of human feelings to witness such usage of even the dumb beasts of the forest.

Nov. 7. To-day there is an interval in the uneasiness of the prisoners. A flag of truce boat is in. It is now thought and earnestly hoped that something will be done to relieve the sufferings of our prisoners, both here and on Belle Isle; yet, what the result will be time only can reveal. It is expected that Col. Wm. Irvine, of the 10th N. Y. Cavalry, will be assistant commissioner of exchange. As we are here incarcerated, not knowing at what hour or at what moment we shall be ushered from time to eternity, we can but think of the thousands who are at home; and when we compare their condition with that of the tens of thousands who have swam the fearful flood, or the many others who have been in the paths of the devastating armies, oh, what thoughts come crowding upon our minds. How many there are who know nothing, comparatively, of the magnitude of the scathing effects of this war. Yes, thousands who are away from the blood stained fields of battle may think it a grievous burden to be obliged to pay a small portion of their earnings for the support of those who value their lives as naught in comparison with the interests of the nation and the integrity of our government. To such I can only say, that whenever they are willing to exchange places let them do so. Let them submit to the wanton cruelty of debased and infuriated men. Let their costly mansions be pillaged and burned; let their property be used for the enemy's subsistence, and their own lives held in jeopardy, then I think that the howling of northern Disunionists would be heard no more.

Nov. 8. For several days past, my health has been very poor. I have had an examination by the prison surgeon and am now in the Libby Prison hospital; last night was a severe one with me. I am afflicted with the scurvy, chronic diarrhœa and fever. These are the prevailing diseases here, and from their baleful effects hundreds of our brave men are dying daily. It is nothing more or less than a charnel house! We are constantly in the midst of the dead and dying. I am well aware that in time of war, on the field of carnage, in camp, where the pestilential fevers rage, or in the crowded prisons of the enemy, under such circumstances human life is but little valued. Yet there are moments amidst all these scenes, when the awful reality seems to force itself upon the mind of every man with power that can not be resisted. In the midst of these scenes, how often, with the poet, can I exclaim:

> "How much is to be done! My hopes and fears
> Start up alarmed, and o'er life's narrow verge
> Look down — on what? A fathomless abyss,
> A dread eternity! how surely mine!
> And can eternity belong to me,
> Poor pensioner on the bounties of an hour?"

Yes, often, when we think not only of our suffering at the hands of the enemy, but of the demoralizing effects upon our characters, we almost despair. But this is not all. There are other thoughts — thoughts of those who are away from these sanguinary fields, but whose minds are turned towards their friends, either in the deadly combat or in the hands of the enemy.

Nov. 9. Passed a very restless, uneasy night — not suffering much to-day from pain, but am very feeble. My blood is in a very bad condition, which is the result of an improper diet.

Nov. 11. I rise this morning weary and fatigued. Sleep was impossible; coughed severely at intervals. Well, I am here, in the hands of merciless and brutal men. I may as well submit without a murmur; for neither complaints nor words of denunciation will avail. I must abide the result, and take my chance with the thousands of others, who, like me, are unfortunate. In the hospital, we have for breakfast, one small slice of bread; for dinner, a table spoonful of rice, and a very small piece of meat; for supper, we have the same allowance as for breakfast. We have no other rations, and are not certain that this scanty portion will be long continued; for we know not what disposition they may finally make of us; but know, however, that they are prepared to do whatever might best advance their own interests. Judging from the treatment that we receive, I think we are warranted in saying that there is no hope of their being restrained by remorse of conscience. They will not be checked in their fiendish designs by the sentiments of humanity.

I would that the principle set forth by the Great Teacher of mankind were introduced into the practical lives of each man and woman. Yes, were we all to "do unto others" as we would that they should "do unto us," I am sure that these sad calamities would not be known.

Nov. 15. I still find myself very weak, but am rather on the gain. There will soon be an exchange of all surgeons who are held as prisoners of war here. There is the wildest excitement imaginable among the gentlemen of that profession. The anxiety, the hopes and fears, all have a strange, a wonderful effect upon them. They are well nigh insane. To-day I received a communication from Lieut. S. H. Tresouthick, 18th Pa. Cavalry, through the key hole of the door which once led from this to the lower east room, where the lieutenant is at present confined. An escape from the prison is contemplated, with what success remains, of course, to be known. My plan of escape, communicated to him, seems to meet with his approbation. We therefore intend to put my scheme into operation as soon as I am sufficiently recovered to be able to endure the fatigue of walking. I am well aware that an escape from prison is attended with much difficulty as well as danger. Even should we succeed in breaking the enclosure, we must necessarily proceed with our lives in our hands. But there is scarcely any risk that we would not gladly subject ourselves to, rather than endure the tortures of prison life. And when placed in such conditions men will appear, to the careless observer, to be almost desperate in their undertakings. We shall hail with rapturous joy the day that we may be permitted to step again within the Union lines. Freed from these toils, we should be able to throw ourselves, heart and hand, against the oppressor's ranks. But,

> "Oppression shall not always reign;
>   There comes a brighter day,
> When freedom, burst from every chain,
>   Shall have triumphant sway.
> Then right shall over might prevail,
>   And truth, like heroes, armed in mail,
> The hosts of tyrant wrong assail,
>   And hold eternal sway."

There has been a world of suffering, in consequence of the oppressor's wrongs. Yet the time will come when these wrongs shall be compensated. The traitor will not go unpunished; and the victim will ultimately find good growing out of evil. All that we can do, is to implicitly trust in the arm of Him, who is the arbiter of all events. So, I have full assurance that somewhere, either in time or eternity, all will be well.

Nov. 23. One month ago I entered this den of torture. The prospect of an immediate exchange having vanished, there seems to be no hope, for at least one or two months to come. We can with but slight certainty predict the future. This is true, under *favorable* circumstances; but in *these* times of doubt and uncertainty, we truly know not what a day may bring forth.

Nov. 24. The exchange of surgeons has finally been accomplished, and there is now a general feeling of joy within the walls of Libby. Although we are still destined to remain, yet it is a source of joy to know that some of our members are afforded the opportunity of leaving these execrable walls. Yet we cannot but think that we shall all be exchanged before long. The surgeons left Libby this morning at about 9 o'clock. Received *The Richmond Sentinel* this evening through the key hole, from a friend up stairs. There is still much talk about exchange. We are all much pleased with the prospect, though dim it be. But the adage is true: "A drowning man will grasp a straw."

Nov. 26. This is thanksgiving day. We, of course, can feel, and indeed are thankful that our condition, even bad as it is, is no worse. The man who lives as he ought, will be thankful for blessings, in whatever form they come. Yes, and if we strive to live as becomes intelligent men, we must be thankful even for adversity; for the Ruler of the universe knows all our wants — is familiar with the complicated circumstances that surround us; and we, the transient beings of earth, can never grasp the designs of the Infinite — cannot say what will tend to our ultimate weal or final woe. True, we will not attempt to judge any one; yet it seems strange that these butchers of men, and murderers of women, should have the hardihood to turn to the God of justice, and, amid all their infamy and crime, with no desire of right, and no thoughts of repentance, implore the bestowal of His blessings upon their deeds of blood. Did they manifest a desire of doing right, of extending the cordial hand of sympathy and brotherhood to earth's afflicted ones, of alleviating the wants and misery of the perishing thousands, then we might have some faith in their prayers. But to see men standing with the iron heel of tyranny placed firm upon the necks of the weak, extend their hands, bathed in fraternal blood, toward the Infinite Father of us all — ah! such deeds of sacrilege will receive their deserved merit. This day has been appointed by President Lincoln as a season for returning thanks to the Father of mercies. There is no danger of its being turned into a day of feasting; for our stinted allowance will not admit of that. Maj. Turner allowed an issue of the remaining few of our private boxes this morning, which have been in his possession for the past two months. They were all broken open, and were generally stripped of everything which could be of any use to us. They were plundered by the common soldiers of the regiment doing guard duty here, under the eyes and with the permission of the prison authorities. Were we among barbarians, such treatment would be nothing more than we might reasonably expect. But among civilized men, who acknowledge that a God of justice rules among the nations of the earth, with the name of Christian ever on their lips, it is not endurable!

Nov. 27. We are now on the commencement of another day. Rain seems to be falling almost in torrents. We understand that a few private boxes will be issued this morning. Yesterday I received a letter from Capt. Poughkeepsie, A. A. I. G. to General Davies. I learn, through him, that the old brigade, to which I was attached when in the field, is now laying near Stevensburgh, Va. I have also received a letter from Uncle Abner Johnson. The reception of these letters, however, is an unusual occurrence; for we are seldom permitted to correspond with our friends; and then only under the most cruel restrictions. Our letters are limited to six lines of ordinary note paper, including date, signature and address. They are carefully criticised by the rebel authorities, and no information concerning our true condition is allowed to be sent. Every scheme that could be divined to outwit the rebels has been resorted to, and successful to some extent; for a large number of prisoners have learned the secret of writing with invisible ink, composed of a mixture of soda and water, which leaves no impression upon the paper until it is heated, when it becomes quite distinct, and may be easily read. But this secret was at length discovered; it occurred in this wise. A captain, writing to a fair and undoubtedly very dear friend, could not brook to be limited to only six lines, when he had so much to communicate; so, resorting to this mixture, he completely filled the sheet with "soft and winning words;" and then, fearing lest his correspondent should not discover the secret, advised his dear Dulcinea to read it, and after baking it to read it again; but the rebels, thinking that if there was to be any baking done that they might as well do it, at once proceeded to heat it, when lo! a blank sheet was at once converted into several close and legibly written pages. You may be assured that our correspondence was most carefully scrutinized, and in the future our letters will, without doubt, be subjected to all manner of tests.

Nov. 28. Some of our senior officers have complained to the prison authorities in relation to our rations, but to no purpose. You might as well approach a granite rock, with expectation of receiving sympathy; for they are perfectly hardened to all feelings of humanity, and are only delighted with the intensity of our sufferings. From the day of our capture dates a sad history of privation and misery, far surpassing in bitter reality anything which the pen of novelist has produced. Rather than to expe rience what we have suffered, there are few men who would not embrace a speedy death. Yes, death would be to them a welcome release.

The ravages of death are spreading most fearfully among our enlisted men on Belle Island, and in the various hospitals of the city. The authorities give no attention to the burial of the dead, except when the keeper of the dead-house cries out to the prison carter, "A load of dead Yankees; drive up your mule." The carter then drives up, and takes in his load with as much unconcern as though he were drawing wood or other articles. It is strange what an effect war and barbarity will have upon the sensibilities of man. Think of the sufferings caused by this most unholy war; think of the vast destruction of life and property; and all this, because the slave autocrats of rebeldom could not rule this nation of freemen unchecked. There is an awful responsibility resting somewhere; and that responsibility, sooner or later, must be met. For an evil, a positive wrong cannot always exist. Upheld by foreign aid, it may for a time seem to bid defiance to truth and justice, but, sooner or later, deprived of its support, it must totter and fall. For,

> "Truth, though crushed to earth, will rise again;
>   The eternal years of God are hers.
> But error, wounded, writhes in pain,
>   And dies amid its worshippers."

Nov. 29. Truly, we know not what an hour may bring forth. I have just received a letter from my mother; but sad! sad, indeed, is the intelligence. The feelings and emotions of this day will long be remembered; for it is the saddest day of all my life. I have just learned, by letter, that my sister Elvira is dead. Her death occurred on the 20th of Oct., the day after my capture. I know this to be the common lot of all; that, sooner or later, without exception, we must go. Yes, we must leave the allurements of earth — friends, at that hour, cannot detain us. This event brings to my mind the passage that has so often lingered there: "How complicate, how wonderful is man!"

> "How passing wonder, He who made him such!
> Who centred in our makes such strange extremes.
> *   *   *   *   *   *
> What can preserve my life! or what destroy?
> An angel's arm can't snatch me from the grave;
> Legions of angels can't confine me there."

GENERAL BRAGG'S DEFEAT.

The rebels are now smarting under the severe defeat of Gen. Bragg; and although desirous of keeping us in ignorance of our success, yet we have been able to gather nearly all of the particulars. It seems that Gen. Hooker, on the 24th, succeeded in carrying, by assault, the northern slope of Lookout Mountain, while Gen. Sherman, coöperating with him, crossed the river at the mouth of the South Chickamauga. After meeting an obstinate resistance, he at last succeeded in capturing the northern extremity of Missionary Ridge. Owing to the combined success of Hooker and Sherman, the enemy abandoned Lookout Mountain during the night, retiring toward Chickamauga. Early the next morning the battle was commenced with renewed energy by Gen. Sherman, who made an assault upon the enemy at the northern end of Missionary Ridge; but our troops met with a severe repulse. The field was hotly contested with varied fortune until 3 o'clock in the afternoon, when Gen. Grant, by hurling two columns against their centre, forced them back and gained possession of the ridge. The enemy, once routed, retired rapidly toward Dalton, Ga., being hotly pressed by our forces as far as Ringold. The rebels admit a loss of six thousand prisoners, seven thousand stand of small arms, and upwards of fifty pieces of artillery.

They regard this as one of the severest defeats that they have sustained since the war began.

Nov. 30. Sadness still lingers around me. The intelligence of yesterday leaves me in very low spirits. The weather is extremely cold, and the sufferings of the prisoners in the upper rooms are indescribable, owing to the inclement weather. There are no fires, and, as yet, there is but little prospect of their being furnished with stoves. Many of our men on Belle Island are dying daily from exposure.

There is still much excitement in relation to Gen. Bragg's defeat. Many rumors are afloat in the papers concerning the extent of his misfortunes.

Dec. 2. The weather is still very cold. The intensest suffering prevails. Many of the prisoners have no blankets, and are poorly clad. They are compelled to walk during the night time to keep from freezing.

This morning we obtained the *Richmond Enquirer* through one of our guards. It is thought that Gen. Meade will soon come in contact with Gen. Lee. Both armies are now drawn up in line of battle, on opposite sides of Mine Run. The rebels seem to be greatly alarmed at the critical state of affairs, and we are most deeply interested in the result of the movement, which we earnestly hope may, in addition to the defeat of Gen. Lee and the capture of Richmond, release us forever from these filthy dungeons.

Dec. 3. This morning I read the *Richmond Sentinel,* which was passed to me through a key hole by friend Richardson. Gen. Meade is reported to be retiring in the direction of Fredericksburg. The object of the movement is not understood here.

A small portion of the clothing sent on by our government is now being issued to the enlisted men on Belle Island. Col. J. M. Sanderson, of our service, is permitted to make the issue. The prisoners are in a state of utter destitution, and the clothing cannot be distributed without guards; the poor boys, having been so long destitute, and having almost perished for the want of sufficient covering, now rush upon the party making the issue, and take such articles as they need. There is no way of keeping them in restraint but by military force. There is much misery here, caused by the disregard of justice. Could all the corruption and consequent suffering be known, it would be a dark spot upon the annals of American history.

Dec. 8. The weather is a little more mild to-day, and I find my health gradually improving. The greater portion of my time is now occupied in reading Napoleon and his marshals.

I make it a daily practice to read the Bible, and to commit a portion of St. Matthew.

There are games of amusement among us, which I sometimes participate in; the most popular are chess, checkers, dominoes, and cards. This evening I had a game of chess with Lieut. Carter, formerly of Baltimore. This was my first attempt at that game, and I am very much pleased with it. Were we in different circumstances, I should not, as a matter of course, approve of devoting to these games time that ought to be more wisely improved. But situated as we are here, anything, not pernicious in itself, that will have a tendency to enlist for a time the attention of the prisoners, seems to have a good effect upon them. Something is needed to cheer and enliven; for where a spirit of despondency settles down upon a man, his death becomes certain. Let his mind be withdrawn, if possible, from the sadness of his condition, and there is relief, an alleviation of his woe, temporarily at least.

AN ESCAPE AND ITS CONSEQUENCES.

Dec. 12. Last night, Capts. Anderson and Skelton made their escape by bribing the guard; in consequence of which there has been several roll calls to-day. The authorities have not yet learned that the guard was bribed. To-day but very little wood has been issued; and our hitherto scanty rations have been reduced as a punishment for the escape of Anderson and Skelton. It seems to be an established custom with Maj. Turner, to punish all the prisoners for the escape of a single man from his number; and we now expect the most cruel exposure to cold and hunger for several days to come. The rebels seem to have no mercy for the sick — no sympathy for the distressed and suffering of the human race. They appear to have no fear of God, nor regard for man.

MY RETURN FROM THE HOSPITAL.

Dec. 16. This morning all who were able to walk were taken from the hospital by order of Gen. Winder. No regard is had for the wounded and sick. Every one who can walk a mile in twenty-four hours is supposed to leave the hospital. Many who are suffering from wounds, and dying with scurvy and other diseases, are positively refused medical treatment, and are thus left like brutes to perish; and this, for no other reason than that there is danger of their making an escape. It is heart-rending to see the sick and wounded treated with such barbarity; driven and compelled to walk, when every step seems to be the last — Great God! deliver me from the hands of cruel men!

Dec. 26. The prisoners confined here are divided into messes of twenty, and a commissary is appointed to each mess, who attends to the issue of rations, and superintends the cooking. Cooks are appointed from the mess, and do duty in rotation.

EXCHANGE RUMORS.

There is much excitement to-day concerning the exchange of prisoners. Many conflicting reports have grown out of Capt. Sawyer's letter from Maj. Mulford. It is rumored that thirty officers and five hundred men are already declared exchanged. There seems to be much hilarity among the prisoners; yet I fear, as has been too often the case, we shall be disappointed. True, we cannot but feel great anxiety for our release; yet such reports have been so often afloat, that I can place but little confidence in anything that may be said in relation to exchange. When we see indications of an actual exchange, then I think it will be quite soon enough for us to rejoice. We can only place an implicit trust in Him who guides and controls the varied events of life.

Dec. 29. A short time since three captains were sentenced to hard labor; and last night, in accordance with that decree, they were ordered out, and will undoubtedly go to Salisbury, N. C.

The event so much desired by all will, in all probability, not transpire, at least, as soon as we could wish, for the exchange, so much talked of, proves only a vain expectation. Thus we are ever the subjects of delusive hopes.

Dec. 31. This day closes up the old year, and soon, if life is spared, we shall enter upon the duties of the new; and what shall be the issues of the coming year none of us can tell. There is an air of sadness observable on the countenances of many, while others, thinking of the festivities of other days, on the occasion of this anniversary, seem desirous of celebrating as they were wont to do in the more peaceful days of yore. Many are making preparations to have a dance in the cook room this evening. Evening advances, and with its onward march the dance ensues. For a time, the prisoners seemed to forget that they were securely enclosed within these inhospitable prison walls. The merriment and hilarity still continued till the old year passed away, to return no more. There was the dance, the lively time and the national song; and these, for a time, appeared to fill the hearts of all with glee.

THE NEW YEAR IN LIBBY.

Jan. 1, 1864. Another year has been ushered in to mark an important period in the world's history. Its records will, ere long, be fixed by the historian, and posterity shall know the successes and defeats, the trials and sufferings of the present eventful epoch. Oh! would, as we are now commencing another year, that the veil of futurity were once removed, that we might read our destiny in the vision of future events. But it is, doubtless, best that we should not know the issues of the future. "Sufficient unto the day is the evil thereof."

Jan. 2. The following is the daily allowance

of rations issued to us by the prison authorities: About three-fourths of a pound of corn bread, one gill of rice, and one-half pound of beef, and a very little salt. On such rations we are left to live or die. Groceries can be purchased of the prison commissary at the following rates:

Potatoes per bushel,	$40 00
Wheat bread, six ounce loaves,	1 00
Butter per pound,	10 00
Lard per pound,	8 00
Sugar per pound,	6 00
Onions per bushel,	50 00
Coffee per pound,	10 00
Tea per pound,	12 00
Eggs per dozen,	6 00

At the above prices the prisoners may purchase the necessaries of life by disposing of their clothing, rings, and anything else of value which it may be their good fortune to possess.

PUNISHMENT FOR SINGING OUR NATIONAL SONGS.

Jan. 24. I went to the cook room last evening for a walk, and there found about sixty prisoners, marching around the room at double quick, in columns of fours. I fell in with them, and all commenced singing *Star Spangled Banner*, *Rally 'Round the Flag Boys*, &c. Maj. Turner (rebel) came in and said, we were a boisterous set of scoundrels. He ordered us into line, and marched us to the north end of the cook room, where we were kept in a standing posture till 10 o'clock P. M. The fires were out early in the evening, and the guards were ordered to fire upon the first one who should attempt to move from the position in which Maj. Turner had placed us. This was the punishment for singing our national songs. The authorities are vigilant and oppressive.

Jan. 28. Twenty-seven of our number are now engaged in digging a tunnel, under the supervision of Col. Thos. E. Rose, 77th Pa. Vol. It is not generally known to the prisoners; for but few beside the working party are, as yet, admitted into the secret. The tunnel starts from the cook room, passes down a chimney into the basement, thence under Cary street, and is designed to terminate in a small yard opposite the prison. A trowel and an old piece of a canteen are the only implements in use. The dirt is taken out in bags and cast into the cellar.

Feb. 10. This day has been almost wholly occupied with roll calls. Maj. Turner reports one hundred and fifteen prisoners missing. The authorities have many wild conjectures concerning the manner of escape. Maj. T. is of the opinion that the guard must have been bribed. Many of the sentinels have been arrested and thrown into "Castle Thunder." As a matter of course, the prisoners feign perfect ignorance as to the method of escape; although it is well known to us that the exit was made through the tunnel, to which we have already alluded. But late in the afternoon the tunnel was discovered by the adjutant of the prison.

Feb. 11. Twelve of the prisoners who made their escape yesterday have been re-captured, and thrown into the cells. The tunnel, through which the escape was made, is regarded a great curiosity by the rebels. Large crowds from town are here to view the wonder.

Feb. 12. Sixteen more of the escaped prisoners were brought in this morning and placed in close confinement. Their rations have been greatly reduced, and many of them have been thrown in irons.

Maj. Turner allowed an issue of boxes to-day, which have been in his hands for the past two months. The scoundrel had given our government the assurance that all private boxes sent on to the prisoners would be immediately distributed; but in this case there is not even "honor among thieves." Most of the boxes were plundered under the eyes of the prison authorities; and those that were issued were robbed of their most valuable contents. Twenty more of the escaped prisoners were brought in to-day.

THE GREAT TUNNEL.

Feb. 24th. The great tunnel which, since the escape of the one hundred, has been the occasion of so much astonishment, so much curiosity, was in process of digging forty-seven days. The work was under the supervision of Col. Rose, of the 77th Pa. Vol. Infantry. The colonel was well prepared to superintend the work, for he had served in the Mexican war, was taken prisoner by the Mexicans, and after a short confinement escaped, by tunnelling from the prison a sufficient distance to be clear from the guards, He had learned his apprenticeship, and was now prepared to manage and direct. None were acquainted with the project but the laborers, those who were engaged in effecting the work.

THE PLAN OF OPERATION.

We had succeeded in removing a number of brick from the side of a large chimney, and by placing a ladder which the rebels had used in raising the prison flag, in the interior of the chimney, we were enabled to descend, and thereby gain access to an unoccupied basement room. This was an under-ground room, having its sides walled up with stone. By removing a few stones from the wall, we were in a situation to commence the process of tunnelling.

CONVENIENCES FOR PERFORMING THE WORK.

The only implements in our possession for performing the work, were an old trowel and half of a canteen. The arduous labor was commenced with the fragment of a canteen, but with this, the progress was so slow, that the most patient were almost disheartened. Fortunately for us, a mason came in to repair the prison walls, and going to dinner before he had finished his work left his trowel, which in his absence most mysteriously disappeared. To him it may have been of but little account, to us it was a God-send. With the aid of this implement, we were able to make more rapid progress, were greatly encouraged, and worked night and day with ceaseless energy. Two of our number were kept in the tunnel almost constantly. One, by a vigorous use of the trowel and canteen, would advance slowly on, placing the dirt in an old blanket, which the other would convey out of the tunnel into a corner of the basement room whence the tunnel started. The work was entirely screened from rebel authorities, as they never had occasion to visit this apartment, and the aperture in the chimney was carefully concealed. We at length succeeded in digging under ground, until we had passed beyond the line of sentinels stationed about the prison, and then worked our way to the surface, leaving a passage just large enough for one man to crawl through at a time.

EACH MAN DETERMINED TO BE FIRST OUT.

The prisoners were then informed of the tunnel, and all were jubilant with the hope of escape, all hands commenced packing up, but egress was so slow that it soon became evident to the cool calculator, that at the best but a comparatively small proportion of our number would be fortunate enough to take their departure from Libby, before daylight would forbid all further attempts to breathe the free air of heaven. Many then became selfish, and thought only of furthering their own wishes; all rushed for the mouth of the tunnel, each man seeming determined to be first out. By this movement, the organization formed by the working party was broken up, and the workmen who were to have had the first opportunity for escape, were not more favorably situated than those who never had borne a hand in the digging. At the mouth of the tunnel were hundreds most eagerly waiting their time. Through the intense anxiety, there was a rush and a crowd, each one being eager to improve his earliest opportunity. Several false alarms occurred, which somewhat retarded the egress; but during the silent hours of night the work went on, yet most slowly indeed, for only one hundred and fifteen of our number were able to effect their escape.

THE ROLL CALL.

In the morning all who remained in Libby were in their places at roll call. The rebels commenced counting us as usual, and noticing the absence of a hundred and fifteen, thought there must have been a mistake in the count. We were re-counted with the same result. We were then all driven into one room, and made to pass through a door one by one, into an adjoining apartment, and were there counted with the same result as at first.

THE GUARD IN CASTLE THUNDER.

The authorities were then exasperated, and knew not how to account for the escape. They first arrested the guard and threw them into Castle Thunder, thinking as a matter of course that they had been bribed. To them it was a mystery almost inexplicable.

Towards night, however, Lateush, the prison adjutant, discovered the dark passage, the tunnel, and this was the greatest wonderment that could have occurred. Word rapidly passed among the rebels; thousands thronged to view the curiosity. It received the name, "The Great Yankee Tunnel." That was the only topic of conversation for a number of days succeeding the escape, it absorbed the attention of all, and was commented upon most largely by the press.

KILPATRICK'S RAID.

March 8. Some of the guard, more communicative than discreet, have been led to disclose all they know conce... ...rning Kilpatrick's raid. It seems, from what we ca... ...n learn, that an expedition has been organized to... ...r the purpose of releasing the prisoners at Rich... ...mond. We have heard the dull booming of artille... ry at intervals during the day, which proves that our troops are already engaging the enemy in the ... fortifications. The prisoners are all on the *qui vive*, anxiously awaiting the result; and *how* anxiously! When, since the commencement of the war, has there been so much at stake? Richmond, to be gained or lost, and with it the freedom of thousands of brave men, incarcerated in filthy dungeons, and dying of starvation!

OUR ORGANIZATION.

We have organized ourselves into regiments, appointed officers, and made all necessary preparation for coöperating with our troops in case of a release, as they are undoubtedly prepared to supply us with arms. The day wears away, and still no change in the situation as we can learn. Night comes, and the welcome sound of artillery has ceased, and all are earnestly inquiring "if it is a repulse, or whether darkness has put an end to a conflict destined to break forth with renewed energy in the morning?"

But the rebels seem as desirous of information. selves, and equally as much in doubt as ourselves, and equally as desirous of information.

March 12. During the last few days, since the battle, we have learned some of the particulars, from rebel sources, concerning the fate of Gen. Kilpatrick's expedition.

It seems that at Frederick's Hall Col. Dahlgren, with about five hundred men, was detached, with orders to move by the way of Louisa Court House, while Kilpatrick, with the main body, moved on Ashland, thus threatening Richmond with two columns, destroying all government property on the line of their march. But a misfortune, which a military commander in an enemy's country is so liable to meet with, thwarted one of the best conceived and most daring plans of the war.

NEGRO GUIDE SHOT FOR PERFIDY.

Col. Dahlgren had employed a negro as guide, who betrayed him by leading in the direction of Gouchland, when Dahlgren discovered his mistake. He ordered the negro to be executed for his perfidy, and, changing his course, commenced marching rapidly upon Richmond; but the rebels were now well informed of the movement, and were on the alert.

DEATH OF COL. DAHLGREN.

On his return, Col. Dahlgren destroyed the Dover flouring mills and several private flouring establishments. He also materially injured the James River canal; but in attempting to cross the river he was surprised by a party in ambush, who fired upon him, killing himself and scattering his party by the first volley.

Kilpatrick, deprived of the valuable services of Dahlgren, and having also to contend against an enemy who were receiving large reinforcements from Pickett's brigade at Bottom Bridge, acted the wise part, and retired during the night in the direction of Mechanicsville.

The advantages gained from the expedition seem to consist wholly in the large destruction of rebel property, and also in cutting the communication between Lee's army and Richmond. The enemy captured a few prisoners, and, of course, claimed a decided victory.

REBEL MODE OF TREATING RAIDERS.

The prisoners captured from the raiding party are treated with the greatest inhumanity.

The rebels evidently have not exhausted all their resources of cruelty upon us; for we are well used in comparison. Officers, enlisted men, and negroes, are crowded together in filthy cells, and not allowed to communicate with the other prisoners. Their rations are much less than ours, and even of a poorer quality; no indignity so great as not to be offered them. At their meals, the officers and negroes are compelled to sit alternately side by side, to prove to our officers in what esteem they are held by the rebels.

The reasons which they assign for this inhuman and uncivilized system of torture, is the destruction of public and private property during the raid, for which they hold them responsible.

METHOD OF COMMUNICATING WITH THE RAIDERS.

The cell in which the raiders are confined is directly underneath my room; of course, every device is used to open communication with them, that we may get a true history of their treatment, and also for the purpose of alleviating their sufferings as much as lies within our power. We have succeeded, by the aid of a saw-backed knife, in cutting a small hole through the door, which we have kept carefully concealed.

Through this hole we have furnished them with a share of such rations as have been issued to us. Some of our number were discovered by the rebels while communicating with them, and, as a punishment for this offence, have been transferred to their cell. Henceforth, this was made the penalty for any such attempt; but its only effect was to warn us to be more cautious in the future.

Thus crowded together in loathsome dungeons, subsisting upon such rations, it is not strange that many of the prisoners are wasting away in death; neither is it strange that foul and malignant diseases are constantly raging amongst us, transferring many rapidly from time to eternity; but all this excites no commiseration from the rebels, for to them it is a fair piece of strategy. Is not the Confederacy being rid of its opposers more rapidly in its prisons, than by any other means which they could devise?

THE PRISON UNDERMINED.

The rebel authorities, fearing that the next attempt at our release might prove more successful than the late effort in our behalf, have adopted a course in perfect harmony with their ideas of civilized warfare. A mine has been dug underneath the prison, and filled with several tons of powder; this we are told is to be sprung in case we endeavor to escape, or if our government should again attempt a release. Such a plan of wholesale murder evinces a state of moral depravity on the part of the authorities at Richmond, to which we challenge the historian to find a parallel in the records of any civilized nation. Can such a people, that will perform acts of this description, without apparent shame or conscious self-abasement, be entitled to be called by the mild term "enemies?" None but the blackest of traitors could resort to such an expedient.

THE SPECIAL EXCHANGE.

March 20. Sixty of our number were paroled to-day, and taken to City Point for the Confederate officers brought down by the Federal authorities; they are to be exchanged. Major McIrvin, of the old regiment, is one of the fortunates. The prisoners are in excellent spirits, and are universally afflicted with "exchange on the brain." Three boat loads have now been permitted to return to God's country, including many of our enlisted men from Belle Isle.

March 22. The officers captured during Kilpatrick's raid are still confined in the cell with negroes, and the officers of colored troops, who have always been treated as felons.

I came very near being detected this morning by Serg't Briggs, while attempting to administer to their wants through the previously described hole in the floor. I had stationed pickets about the building to warn me of the approach of the authorities, but the sergeant happened to be in the small room occupied by Gen. Scammon, at the time I opened the hole, and hence the reason that he was not seen by the men who were on the alert for him; upon leaving the general's room, he passed within six feet of the spot where I was so busily engaged in putting down corn bread, that I did not notice his presence; fortunately, however, several prisoners who were watching me, stepped up as the sergeant passed, and interposed themselves between myself and him, thus saving me from sharing the fate of those whose sufferings I have endeavored to lessen, by supplying them with the necessaries of life.

PRISONERS FROM PLYMOUTH.

April 25. Our number has been increased to-day, by the arrival of several "Fresh Fish," captured recently at Plymouth. Having been employed since their enlistment at that point, they feel their deprivations and hardships much more than the prisoners in general, for the long and fatiguing marches, and the necessary hardships of many campaigns, have somewhat prepared us for greater endurance, and then in the field one learns many expedients for getting along, unknown to a more civilized mode of life.

It was quite amusing to see how the "Pilgrims" regarded their "position." Having prepared their first rations in Libby, which however poor they might be, their long march had made acceptable to them; they remarked, that there was no suitable place for taking their meals, and were not a little embarrassed at the merriment the remark produced among the old prisoners, who had long ceased to consider where they should eat, but what? The want of bunks, and chairs too, gave them equal solicitude, and indeed, we who had been long

Interior View of Libby Prison.

incarcerated, seemed by our tattered garments and disordered appearance more fit subjects for such treatment, and more in harmony with our surroundings.

Through the new arrivals, we are enabled to learn some news from our armies, and the particulars of the fight in which they were captured.

It appears that they were overpowered at Plymouth, and after repelling several desperate charges, were compelled to surrender. Brig. Gen. W. H. Wessells was in command of the post.

April 26. Weather cold and disagreeable. No wood allowed in the upper rooms. Suffering intense. Our men on Belle Island are being removed to Georgia. Exchange stock low.

April 27. Communicated with friends in the hospital this afternoon through a knot hole in the floor. My friend Calhoun not expected to live, he is afflicted with Pneumonia.

April 28. Exchange stock up. It is rumored that there is another "boat up" with prisoners from the north. The terms for a general exchange are said to have been agreed upon, Aiken's Landing being declared the point of execution.

April 30. The prisoners are very despondent

to-day. The rumors of the 28th inst. appear to have had no foundation. The feelings occasioned by our disappointment can be better imagined than described, but imagination, even in her most extravagant flights, can but poorly picture the horrors of this prison life. Our constant experience is "Hope Deferred."

GEN. LEE REPORTED TO BE DEFEATED.

May 6. There had been great excitement in the city during the day concerning war matters.

Gen. Lee was reported to have been defeated, and to be falling back to the fortifications.

Several regiments passed through town in the afternoon, on their way to the front.

At 11 o'clock P. M., we were notified by Major Turner, that we would leave the prison in one hour from that time; and at 12 o'clock, the adjutant's clerk, Mr. Ross, commenced calling the roll. As his name was called, each prisoner passed from the cook room, through the door opening on Cary street, and filed down between two lines of guards, closing up to those who had preceded him, and receiving, as he took his place in the ranks, a "*corn dodger*," which we were told must satisfy hunger until another issue could be made. I could not help rejoicing at my exit from the walls of Libby, for I felt that our condition could be made no worse, while a change of base might present opportunities for escape.

FAREWELL TO LIBBY.

A few of the prisoners were inclined to be despondent, and seemed to endorse the old maxim of "Better bare those ills we have, than fly to others that we know not of." We did not leave Cary street until the dawn of day, when we moved down to the first bridge and crossed over the "James" to Manchester, where we were packed into cattle cars, and started for the south. Our place of destination was not known, but supposed to have been some point in Georgia.

CHAPTER IV.

ARRIVAL AT DANVILLE, VA.

May 7, 1864. It is now late in the evening. We are securely stowed away in cattle cars. The train has just stopped, and we are to remain in our present situation until morning, when we are informed by the rebel authorities here that we shall be removed to the military prison in town. We have had a most disagreeable time on our way from Richmond. The cars were anything but clean, being occupied one day for the transportation of cattle, and the very next, perhaps, for carrying prisoners into the interior of rebeldom, there to endure new hardships.

ESCAPE FROM THE CARS.

Several of our number effected an escape from the train during the fore part of the night. My old friend Barse jumped from his car while in motion. Twenty shots were fired after him by the guard. It is yet uncertain as to whether he escaped unharmed or not. The rebels boast, however, that the d—d Yank will never attempt to make his escape again.

Many others attempted to release themselves in various ways. Some succeeded through the aid of saw-backed knives in hacking holes in the sides of the cars, and then, at the earliest opportunity, made their way out.

The party with whom I was confined were engaged in this manner, but, unfortunately, our work was discovered before its completion; and thus the scheme was exposed. We were not, however, easily discouraged; for what idea will not awaken itself in the mind of man when destined to a loathsome imprisonment?

NEW PLANS FOR ESCAPE.

No sooner was our work discovered, and guards stationed near it, than we began to concoct a new plan for escape; which was to disarm the stupid guard by removing the caps from their guns, and then to dash past them at the first convenient opportunity.

We succeeded in rendering one gun useless; but the guard carrying the other, being on the alert, it was impossible to uncap it, and, consequently, we very reluctantly abandoned our cherished project, and turned to think, or perchance to dream, of "prison pens," "bare feet," "corn dodgers" and "dead lines."

C. S. MILITARY PRISON, DANVILLE, VA.

May 9. After a sleepless night, spent in the cattle cars, we were removed at an early hour this morning to the military prison in town.

The heat is very oppressive to-day. No rain has fallen since the first of the month.

Our daily allowance of rations at this prison is as follows: One loaf of corn bread, weighing about three-fourths of a pound; one-half pound of bacon, and one pint of soup. No other varieties.

There is great suffering for want of room. It is impossible to find a place to sleep without disturbing some one.

We are fired upon by the guard for the offence of looking out of the windows, as was the case at Libby Prison.

I cannot see that anything has been gained by the change; for we meet the same stamp of men here that we left at Richmond.

Danville is situated at the terminus of the

Richmond and Danville railroad, one hundred and forty miles south of the former place, and four miles from the southern boundary of the state. It can be easily defended, and is, without doubt, one of the strongest natural positions south of Richmond. It has a population of about two thousand inhabitants.

There are three large brick buildings on the east side of the town, now in use as military prisons. Previous to our transfer to this place, they were occupied by enlisted men. Near the centre of the second floor of one of these prisons, my messmates, Lieuts. Nyce and Richardson, of the old regiment, and myself, have chosen a small spot, which we call our portion of the room.

SLEEPING SPOON FASHION.

At night we find it necessary to sleep spoon fashion; for, at the best, large numbers are compelled to sit up until morning, and then take the places which others have left. The cry of "spoon to the right or left" is a signal for each individual to turn in the direction indicated by the speaker.

There is no military force at this point, save the prison guard, which is commanded by Maj.

Moffitt, who also acts as commandant of the post.

We learn by rumor that there has been a pretty severe engagement between Grant and Lee since the 7th instant. It is generally inferred, by the uneasiness of the rebels, as well as their disposition to curtail our privileges, that "Uncle Bob," as they familiarly call Gen. Lee, has come off second best.

May 11. A large tunnel is now in process of digging, and, should we remain here another week, we will give the rebels a subject for reflection. The mind naturally reverts to the army, to home and friends; and it is our constant study to invent some scheme by means of which we may be released. Could we but hear from our army, or were we allowed to receive letters, it would be some satisfaction; but no! even this small favor is denied.

One day's rations were issued in advance this morning. We are expecting to be sent farther south. And thus we are kept constantly moving into the interior of rebeldom. The papers are not allowed in prison; but it is the prevailing impression among the prisoners that Gen. Averill is making a raid in this direction; and hence the reason of the uneasiness on the part of the rebels, and their avowed intention to send us to Georgia.

We are all in high glee over the possibilities of a release. Groups are collecting, and talking over the chances of success. Were so many children assembled together in anticipation of a day of jubilee, the scene could not be more wild.

The Star Spangled Banner has just been struck up, and all join heart and soul in singing it.

FROM DANVILLE TO MACON.

In Cattle Cars, near Greensboro, N. C., }
Thursday,—*May* 12. }

At 4 o'clock this A. M. we were marched out of the prison at Danville, and again set in motion toward the south. We think traveling very beneficial to the health; and one not acquainted with the rebel mode of treating prisoners, might be inclined to think that they are disposed to favor us in this respect; for we do not seem destined to remain in one place any great length of time.

It is raining now. There is a damp, chilly air, which is anything but agreeable; and our meager shelter is but little better than none at all, as a protection from the storm. The wind drives the rain into the sides of the cars; and then, too, the roof is not water proof.

CONSCRIPTS FOR LEE'S ARMY.

The rebels are apparently very much alarmed at the state of affairs in *Northern Virginia*. We met conscripts almost every hour on their way to join Gen. Lee's forces. After a ride of twenty-four miles by rail, we were compelled to leave the cars, and march on foot to within eight miles of this place.

The roads were muddy, and our tramp by no means pleasant; for our long imprisonment and scant rations have rendered us completely unfit for a walk of half a mile even. We suffered much in attempting to keep pace with the guard, who urged us forward at the point of the bayonet, cursing and threatening most fearfully all those that fell by the way from weakness and utter exhaustion. As yet, there have been no opportunities for escape. The guard is very vigilant. No prisoner is allowed outside of the cars, on penalty of being shot.

AN ATTEMPT TO ESCAPE.

I attempted an escape this evening, before we were put into the cars, by hiding behind a rail fence, but was discovered and driven from my place of concealment. I endeavor to think that all things are for the best; and my present seeming ill success is perhaps a blessing in disguise; for had I succeeded in escaping the vigilance of the guard, I might have fallen into worse hands were such a thing possible.

We often feel grieved and sad over the calamities and disappointments incidental to this life; but could we look from a broader stand point, we might see that the afflictions of to-day, however severe, are the greatest favors that infinite wisdom could confer upon us. There is a Divinity that shapes our ends, rough hew them as we will.

Near Charlotte, N. C.,
Friday,—*May* 13.

Having left Greensboro early this morning, we reached Charlotte late in the afternoon, and were marched, under heavy guard, to the Commons. We are told that an issue of rations will be made before leaving this place.

ENTERTAINING CITIZENS.

On learning that there were Yankee prisoners in town, the citizens came out in large numbers. Many approached the guard line, and endeavored to converse with us, but were forced back at the point of the bayonet. We have been entertaining our visitors by singing the *Star Spangled Banner*, *Rally Round the Flag Boys*, and several other national airs.

I observed many white handkerchiefs fluttering in the breeze during the singing, expressive of "loyalty" and delight, no doubt, at their good fortune in being permitted to hear what they would not dare give utterance to themselves.

The rebel officer in command became so much enraged at their friendly bearing toward us, that he ordered out a detail to drive them from the ground.

PLANS FOR ESCAPE.

There has been much speculation among the prisoners, since our arrival here, upon different plans of escape; being fully satisfied, that if we can but pass from the hands of the guard that we shall find little difficulty in reaching our lines, aided by the loyal citizens, as we may very naturally expect to be.

It is now getting dark, and the guard is being doubled. No rations have yet been issued. I see nothing that indicates a move from this place before morning.

Columbia, South Carolina,
Saturday,—*May* 14.

We left Charlotte, under very exciting circumstances, at 1 o'clock this morning.

The night being dark, and the soil light, many of the prisoners dug holes in the ground and there buried themselves, hoping thus to escape the vigilance of the guard, when we should be marched from the field to the cars. Unfortunately, however, the scheme was exposed by one of the guards, who accidentally stumbled into a hole, in the bottom of which he beheld a live Yankee.

Struck with astonishment, he shouted, "O my God! captain, here be one Yank bury heself in the ground!" A great excitement was the natural consequence. A general search ensued. Torchlights were used and the trees and ground thoroughly inspected. This investigation brought to light several holes of a similar character, each having deposited therein a Federal prisoner. Our liberties were immediately curtailed, and after hurriedly driving us into the cars, we were again set in motion toward the south. This place was reached late in the afternoon. We are to make a brief halt here, and then, as we understand, move on to Macon, Ga.

Augusta, Georgia, Sunday,—May 15.

Reached town at six o'clock this P. M., and were turned over to the city militia, a motley crowd of cowardly ruffians, who seem to think that to be soldierly they must abuse a defenceless prisoner whenever the simplest pretext can be found.

The suffering caused by close confinement is most intense. We have not been permitted to leave these filthy cattle cars since our adventure at Charlotte, and I can see no prospect of it before we arrive at our place of destination.

The son[*] of Gov. Bradford, of Maryland, is the provost marshal of the city

---

[*] This unprincipled youth afterwards led a band of guerrillas to his father's residence, and with them sacked his former home.

It is still rumored, that we are to be sent to Macon. In all probability, the rebels intend to place us beyond the reach of assistance or rescue, and for aught I know, they may possibly succeed in their attempt.

CHAPTER V.

AT MACON, GA., CAMP OGLETHORPE.

May 17, 1864. Having left Augusta late in the afternoon yesterday, we reached Macon at eight o'clock this morning.

Since leaving Richmond my health has been very poor, caused doubtless, by the various changes to which we have been subjected. At times we were packed in filthy cattle cars at the rate of sixty to a car. The doors were securely closed, in consequence of which, we suffered much for the want of sufficient air. At other times we were in open cars, exposed to the storm and all the inclemencies of the weather. Several of the prisoners escaped from the train.

MACON, ITS MILITARY IMPORTANCE.

May 18. Macon is situated on the Ocmulgee river, in the northern part of the state. It has a population of about ten thousand inhabitants.

It is finely located, and at present is one of the most stirring and important towns in the south. Its distance from Augusta is one hundred and sixty miles, and one hundred miles from Atlanta.

Two papers are published at this place, viz: *The Macon Confederate* and *The Macon Telegraph.*

MAJOR TURNER AT MACON.

On our arrival here at the prison pen, whom should we find but Maj. Thomas P. Turner, the fiend incarnate from Libby Prison. This human (?) monster stood at the gate to count us as we passed in. To his astonishment, forty-seven of our original number were missing, all of whom escaped from the cars.

The insufferable den in which we are confined is about eighty rods east of the city, and embraces a little more than two acres of ground, enclosed by a high stockade fence, within which is the dead line,* about sixteen feet distant from the stockade. It is denomi-

---

* It is an ordinary picket fence, three and a half feet high. In many prison pens of the south it is only a line of stakes, and sometimes a single board nailed to posts.

nated the "dead line," as it marks the limits of the camp; and any attempt to cross it is death, or at least a shot from the guard.

NEW ARRIVALS.

May 20. This morning, one hundred and seven officers from Gen. Grant's army arrived here, to take up their abode in the prison pen. Among the number are Generals Shayler and Seymour. The "fresh fish"* give us much information respecting the movements of our armies.

There are at present about twelve hundred of our officers confined here, four hundred of whom were captured since the commencement of the campaign in front of Richmond.

FIRING UPON A PRISONER.

Lieutenant H. P. Barker, 1st R. I. Cavalry, was fired upon this morning by one of the sentinels, a boy not more than fourteen years old. It is alleged by the guard, that Lieut. B. had his

---

* The first six months of prison life, one is called a "Fresh Fish;" the next four months, a "Sucker;" the next two months, a "Dry Cod;" the balance of his time, a "Dried Herring;" and after exchange, a "Pickled Sardine."

hands on the "dead line," though it is a well known fact that he was not within 16 feet of it.

The authorities have not, as yet, provided us with quarters. A few of the prisoners have blankets, which they use for a shelter; but most of our number have no means of protecting themselves from the scorching sun or the inhospitable storm.

May 22. Our daily allowance of rations at this pen is as follows: Corn meal, one pint; bacon, one fourth of a lb.; rice, one oz.; peas or beans, one oz.; salt, one table-spoonful for four days.

We have no cooking utensils except a few iron skillets. The beans furnished here are wholly unfit for use. The rations issued are about one half of what we really need.

In this prison, and also at Andersonville, the mortality is fearful. Hundreds, yes, thousands starved, murdered by cruel tyrants. The meagre fare, exposure to the inclemency of the weather, and necessary inactivity, are the causes of such frightful consequences.

It is hard to witness the inroads of death, and its ravages, even when skill and care are given to the dying,—it is hard to stand by the death bed, and there witness the last ebbing of life as it departs, leaving behind the inanimate clod of earth. But what is this compared with death in its most ghastly form, by starvation, by exposure to the inclement atmosphere, and by every kind of inhuman treatment. Each day death calls for an hundred,— a hundred at a blow.

May 29. This morning we received notice from the rebel authorities, through Capt. W. Kemp Tabb, present commandant of the prison, that in the future, all prisoners not in ranks at roll call, will be shot down by the sentinels on the guard line. We have also received orders to take our boards and blankets from the ground. The probable reason of this vigilance is, that they have discovered several tunnels which we had commenced, and were carrying forward as fast as possible.

Our plan of operation was as follows: select a bunk in some shed near the "dead line;" sink a hole or "well" as we termed it, straight down to the depth of five or six feet, then start the tunnel proper towards the stockade, under which it passed.

But one man could dig at a time, and as the work was very fatiguing, we relieved each other often.

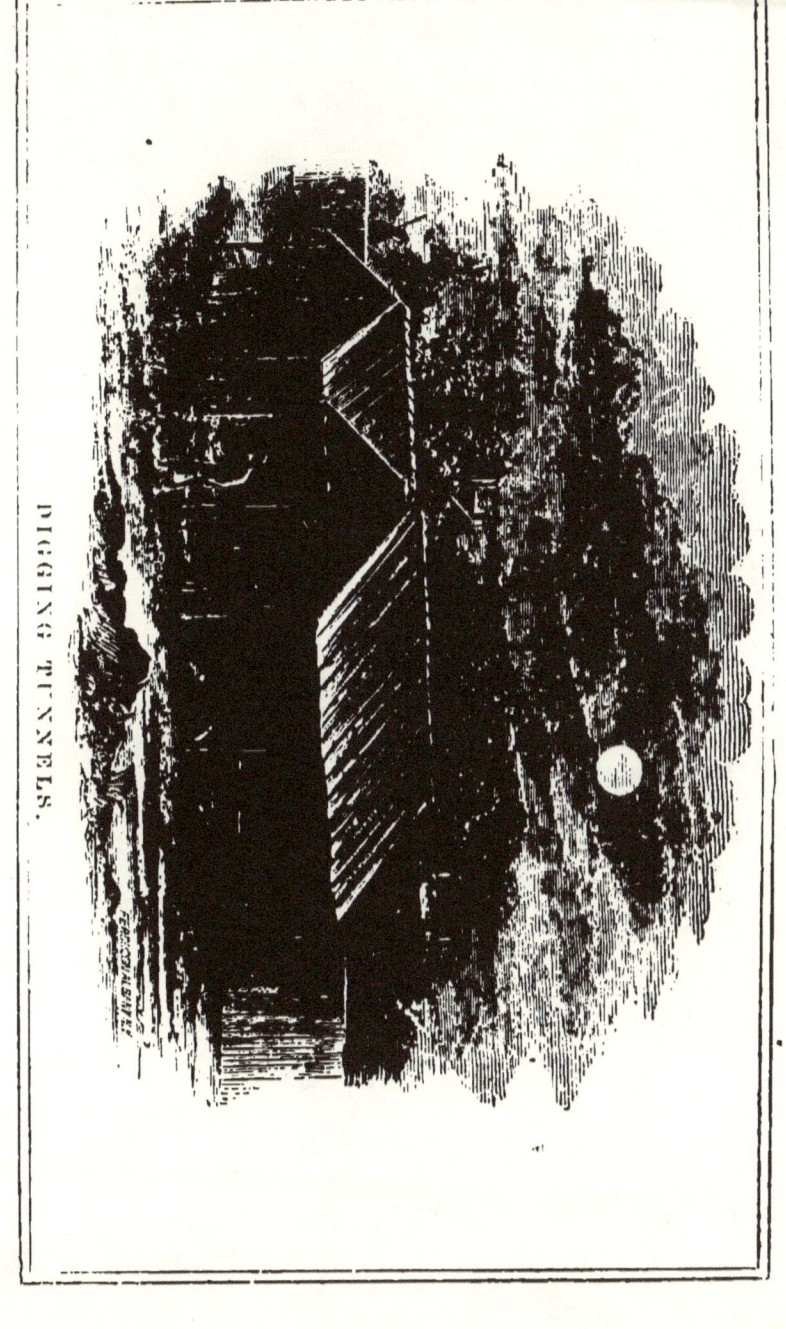

DIGGING TUNNELS.

The dirt was brought to the mouth of the hole in meal sacks, which had been stolen from the ration wagon.

Two or three were detailed to carry off the dirt to the sinks.

We usually commenced operations after ten o'clock in the evening, and continued until nearly daylight.

Upon leaving the tunnel, a board was fitted in about a foot from the surface, and then dirt was swept over so as to obliterate all traces of the digging.

From sixteen to twenty days were thus required to finish the narrow road to liberty. Fires were built by the guard at short intervals, between the dead line and stockade, completely encircling the camp, so that the tunnels had to be carried a great distance, in order to have the place of egress as safe as possible.

If the work could have been completed, we should have chosen some dark and stormy night to remove the slight cap of earth, at the outer extremity of the subterranean channel, and then stealing out cautiously; so as not to attract the attention of the vigilant sentinel, we would have made for the woods and swamps.

Those who had done the digging, were to have had the first opportunity to pass out, and then as many more were to go, as could get through the tunnel before daybreak.

Our plan was a good one, and we felt confident that it would prove a perfect success, until the eve of its completion, when either some cowardly traitor in our midst, or a detective sent in by the authorities, exposed the scheme, and thus blighted our brilliant prospects.

UNPLEASANT CONSEQUENCES.

The result of this attempt to reach "God's country," is a reduction of rations, and a resort to every restriction which could possibly be conceived by a rebel.

While in Libby, I imagined that the deeds of villainy were well nigh exhausted,—I had thought that the catalogue of crime was nearly filled by the Confederate miscreants, but alas! you have only to see the heartlessness and the intrigues of the authorities here,—you have only to witness the suffering, the frenzy and the fever, and you will then say, that these are the deeds of pitiless monsters.

The machinations of cruelty are still permitted

to go on, and the deeds of villainy are yet perpetrated against the Union prisoners. We may well exclaim, How long? oh! how long, shall this continue?

MURDER OF LIEUT. GRIERSON.

June 11. At 9 o'clock this evening, Lieut. Otto Crierson, 95th N. Y. Vols., was shot and mortally wounded by a sentinel on the stockade. It is asserted by the sentinel, that the lieutenant was in the act of making his escape, by crawling up the creek to the "dead line," preparatory to passing under the stockade; but those who were near by, and saw the affair as it occurred, said that he was not in the creek at all, and that he was at least sixteen feet from the "fatal line."

The lieutenant was at the spring where we are accustomed to bathe, and while there for that purpose, was murdered by the wretch, whose name we have not yet learned. We shall mark him if we are ever permitted to catch a glimpse of his cowardly phiz in daylight. I had just left the spring with water, previous to the discharge of the sentry's musket.

We called upon Capt. Gibbs, the prison commandant, informed him of the facts, and requested an investigation, but were turned away with no satisfactory answer, or rather with the understanding, that we need not expect anything in that direction. But the villain who perpetrated the deed was promoted to a sergeant, and given a furlough, for his fidelity and promptness in the execution of orders.

Here goes another of our number, murdered in cold blood, at the hands of a traitor.

June 22. Capt. Gibbs proposes to allow us the privilege, as he is pleased to term it, of choosing delegates to solicit of the authorities at Richmond an opportunity to visit our enlisted men at Andersonville, for the purpose of reporting their condition to our authorities at Washington.*

The fact is, if the truth were known, the rebels seem desirous of placing a weapon in the hands of the peace party at the north, whereby the cause of the Unionists may be defeated.

Confederate officers and citizens are allowed to visit us frequently. They represent to us, and would gladly have us believe, that they are

---

* The representations they propose to make are, "that the awful suffering of our men in southern prisons is caused by a change of climate and the hopelessness of exchange."

doing all in their power to make our situation comfortable and agreeable.

They repeatedly affirm that the non-exchange of prisoners is due entirely to the fault of our government. In short, they are very anxious to have us send a deputation to Washington, for the purpose of placing before President Lincoln and the administration the horrid condition of our men in southern prisons, and to ask an immediate general exchange of prisoners, claiming, as a matter of course, that they are doing all they possibly can for us.

In accordance with their entreaties, we have held a meeting, but the result is quite unsatisfactory to the rebels; for we have most firmly resolved never to become agents in advancing the interests of the southern cause, even though our sufferings be increased a hundred fold.

I am perfectly satisfied that there has been no time since the beginning of the war when the rebels could not have given their prisoners an abundance of corn meal and bacon, were they so disposed; and from observation I know that they could have furnished lumber, to provide us with more comfortable quarters. With such facts, glaring and palpable as they are, could we, as men, yield to their base intrigues to further their fiendish designs? No! not while reason holds her sway.

NEW TUNNELS.

The camp was searched to-day by order of the prison commandant, and the three tunnels which have been in process of digging for the past fifteen days were discovered. Had it not been for this misfortune, many of us would have bid farewell to-morrow night to this field of suffering.

Doubtless some detective from the outside exposed the scheme. Never was I more disappointed than in this misfortune; for our plan was a good one. The tunnels were large, and it was estimated that nearly, if not quite all of the prisoners could pass through them in a single night.

We had looked forward with the deepest anxiety to what we felt assured would be the happy termination of our labors; but alas! when it seemed that we were about to reap the promised reward, like the mirage, it vanished in the distance.

The following order appears upon the bulletin board this morning:

C. S. MILITARY PRISON, MACON, GA.,
June 27th, 1864.

SPECIAL ORDER No. 9.

Sentinels are instructed to shoot down all prisoners in the future who are seen moving about camp after tapps.

GEO. C. GIBBS,
Captain Commanding.

The guards appear delighted to receive orders of such a character, and seem to find real consolation in having the privilege of firing upon us on the most trivial pretext.

Insatiate cormorants! for I cannot use a more appropriate term. A thirst for blood seems to characterize their conduct. But this is no more than might be expected from those who had the nurture and training that they have had. For an oligarchy, founded on slavery as its chief corner stone, must engender characters fully prepared to commit the darkest crime that may threaten a nation's life, trained up from youth to tyrannize over a degraded people. They have no sense of justice, founded deep in the principles of human nature.

SCURVY.

Scurvy is now becoming fearfully prevalent in our midst. Chronic diarrhœa is also sweeping off its victims by tens and twenties. It is almost impossible to get treatment for either. Large numbers, who are afflicted with the former disease, may be seen every day burying themselves up in the ground, as the earth has a tendency to check its frightful ravages.

Much to my disgust, I found, on the morning of the 25th, that this loathsome affliction had at last got hold of me. I had been hoping that it would pass me by in its visitations, but it is unquestionably present in my limbs. I attended sick call this morning, and was prescribed for by the surgeon the first time since we left Richmond. I shall not make any effort to get into the hospital, for I am confident that it is much better to remain in camp, among my friends, where they can administer to my wants, than to go where the prisoner can expect but little sympathy, or anything else that might have a tendency to rid him of disease or recruit his wasted strength.

It is not strange that the term *hospital* has

become synonymous with death; for but few who enter it ever come out alive. When a man is seen leaving camp in a blanket, it is thought that he is past help; and if he is fortunate enough to return to his fellows, it is considered an exceptional case.

Deaths have been very frequent since the warm weather came on. Several went to their long homes last night. We call it being "exchanged;" and it certainly is a happy transformation from so much misery and wretchedness on earth to a life of eternal joy in the bright realms above. We cannot sigh for such, but only rejoice that their cares and misfortunes are ended. It is not wonderful that they should feel, in their last moments, that

"I would not live alway — I joy in the trust,
That when this frail form shall return to the dust,
My spirit shall rise on the wings of thy love,
To seek its true home in the mansions above."

FOURTH OF JULY.—OUR CELEBRATION.

We had several roll calls this morning. The prison authorities seem to be very fearful lest we attempt a general escape.

Immediately after the roll call a large meeting was organized. Captain Todd, 8th New Jersey

Infantry, displayed a small silk flag four by six inches, which had been presented to him by Miss Paradise, of Jersey City, and which had thus far escaped the vigilance of southern relic seekers. The miniature "Star Spangled Banner" was hailed with rounds of cheers, which showed that they came from loyal hearts.

We then adjourned to the large building occupied by the general and field officers, where Chaplain Dixon, 16th Connecticut Volunteers, opened the exercises with prayer. Capt. Ives, Lieut. Ogden, 1st Wisconsin Cavalry; Capt. Lee, 5th Michigan Cavalry; Lieut. Kellogg, Chaplain Whitney, 104th Ohio; Chaplain Dixon, and Lieut. Col. Thorpe, 1st New York Dragoons, then followed with speeches and toasts, interspersed with national songs, while far above our heads, attached to a long pole was the emblem of freedom, the "Red, White and Blue."

Although in prison, and held here by those who ought always to have regarded the people of the north with a brotherly kindness, who never should have raised the recreant hand of treason against the government established by our common fathers and sealed with their blood, yet, under these circumstances even, we could not repress the feelings which spontaneously arose in every breast. No! we shall celebrate with joy the propitious day when we eluded the British Lion.

We shall celebrate that glorious day and "live or die, survive or perish," we shall give a hearty support to those stars and stripes — the banner of the free, that has so long waved over our heads, and for which we are now contending.

Whilst we were listening to a spirited oration from Col. Thorpe, appropriate to the day, whose voice was only heard by those within the prison walls, where no treason could be uttered that might be so regarded by the outside Confederate partisans; yet in the exercise of his "little brief authority," the rebel commandant of the prison, Capt. Gibbs, deemed it necessary to march in a regiment of troops, ordering the assemblage to disperse, which was accordingly done. This is a fair specimen of Southern Chivalry carried out.

Col. Thorpe having been for some time past in command of the interior of the camp, by virtue of his being the senior officer here, was relieved from duty by the following order:

C. S. MILITARY PRISON, MACON, GA.,
July 4th, 1864.

SPECIAL ORDERS No. 6.

I. Lieut. Col. Thorpe is relieved from duty as senior officer of this prison, for a violation of prison rules, and Lieut. Col. McCrary will again assume that position.

II. The same order and quiet will be observed on this day as on any other.

III. A disregard to this order may subject offenders to unpleasant consequences.

GEO. C. GIBBS,
Captain Commanding.

SKIRMISHING.

It matters but little how delicate an officer may have been at first, in his views of such an apparently loathsome operation in the presence of others, he becomes reconciled after a brief sojourn in a southern military prison.

The cars, camps, and prison pens are literally alive with the little "grey backs;" and it is only by a constant and thorough examination of under clothing that one can possibly find rest from their personal attacks.

Hot water and soap kills them; but the latter is issued in such small quantities, and so seldom, as to be of but little avail.

Again we have no conveniences for heating water, save the small kettles, which a few of the prisoners are fortunate enough to possess for cooking purposes.

Still another, and our greatest difficulty is want of a sufficient amount of clothing.

What little was spared us of our former wardrobes, at the time of capture, has been worn out during a long imprisonment.

Washerwomen know that rubbing old garments hurries them to an irreparable dissolution; and prisoners of war have learned the same fact.

Therefore, as a matter of economy, we seldom wash our clothing; and then only to prevent filth.

> Tell me not, in mournful number,
> Prison life is but a dream;
> 'Tis but little we can slumber—
> Swarms of lice in every seam.

July 6. Heat intense. No rain since the early part of last month. I am suffering with chronic diarrhœa at present, but shall not endeavor to get into the hospital while I have a friend left in camp.

July 7. I am no better to-day. Have not tasted of my rations since the fifth.

July 8. Crawled down to the creek in the forenoon, near which I lay until evening.

A fellow prisoner recommended me to chew white oak bark for my complaint, and has persuaded me to try the experiment. He has very kindly placed three pieces of the said bark at my disposal, which he stripped from an old tree that stands within the enclosure.

July 9. I am very weak to-day; cannot walk without assistance. Am inclined to think that chewing bark will not effect a cure in my case.

July 12. I am still very low with chronic diarrhœa, but think I shall recover, as my health seems to be improving at present.

THE AUTHOR SELLS HIS BUTTONS TO SAVE LIFE.

Brass buttons being in great demand with the rebels, I pulled the remaining few from my old coat yesterday, and sold them to one of the guards for ten dollars, and with that sum purchased five loaves of wheat bread, which will last me six or seven days if used sparingly.

I have not touched my corn meal for a long time, my stomach being entirely too weak to endure such a coarse diet, and the consequence is, that I am reduced by starvation to a mere skeleton.

I think that my flour bread will have the desired effect of checking my summer complaint, and recruiting my strength.

I should have disposed of my buttons long ere this, had I not thought that I might see a day of greater need, but decided at last, that if I would remain above the sod, that I must part with my reserves, and considered myself exceedingly fortunate in finding a ready purchaser.

My friends have been very kind during my illness, and are still untiring in their efforts to keep me among the living.

July 16. Health improving. It is affirmed by the authorities, that there will be a general exchange of prisoners on the 24th of the present month. The "fresh fish" are troubled with an affliction known to the old prisoners as "exchange on the brain."

July 27. Six hundred prisoners were counted out of the enclosure this evening; their destination supposed to be Charleston, where they will doubtless be placed under fire of our guns on Morris Island, as were the field officers sent thither during the early part of last month.

This is a most singular method of defending a besieged city against its enemies, and illustrates, to some extent, the character of a people that would like to be "let alone," while attempting to establish a government in accordance with their own chivalrous notions of justice, equality and state rights.

What a mask they would make of religion, by invoking Divine aid in the prosecution of their accursed designs.

The poet's admonition seems to have been forgotten:

> "Beware, ye slaves of vice and infamy.
> Beware — choose not religion's sacred name,
> To sanctify your crimes — your falsehood shield.
> Profane not your Creator's boundless power —
> Or lest his vengeance fall upon, and crush ye.
> It is an awful height of human pride,
> When men dare robe themselves in sanctity,
> While all is dark within!
> This, surely, is the aggregate of sin;
> The last — to be forgiven, by Heaven, or man."

Maj. Cooke, Capt. Downing, Lieuts. Nyce, Shaeffer and Hopper, of the old regiment, are included in the number sent to Charleston. Lieut. Richardson is still with me.

July 28. The second six hundred were counted out of the pen late in the afternoon.

As his name was called, each prisoner stepped between the dead line and stockade, where we expect to remain until morning, when it is generally understood that we will be shipped to the coast.

CHAPTER VI.

AT SAVANNAH, GA., CAMP DAVIDSON.

July 29, 1864. We left Macon at 4 o'clock A. M., guarded by the 5th Ga. Reserves. We were packed into cattle cars at the usual rates. Our treatment at the hands of the guard, however, was much better than on our former jaunts of this kind.

From the hurried and excited manner of the rebel authorities, all, evidently, was not well with them. Artillery was being rapidly hurled into position, the troops were on the alert, and every preparation made to defend the place; but as for ourselves, we could only hope that through their misfortune we might find an opportunity for escape; and the reader may imagine our disappointment when we learned afterwards, from one of the guards, that our cavalry under Gen. Stoneman cut the road at

Griffin Station, only thirty minutes after we had passed.

To think that freedom had come almost within our grasp, and yet eluded us, tended only to add bitterness to our hard lot.

July 30. Savannah is situated on the Savannah river, in the eastern part of Georgia. It is unsurpassed by any other city in the state in its business facilities, and also in its neatness and regularity.

In a military point of view, it stands next to Charleston in importance.

Its population at present is about twenty thousand, including a large number of refugees. The inhabitants are generally suffering from the most abject poverty.

At present there is a perfect stagnation in business; but one can easily judge its past enterprising spirit by the unmistakable marks of its former prosperity.

Our camp is in the eastern part of the city, near the Marine Hospital, which was built and formerly used by our government.

Pulaski's monument stands within plain view.

There are about four thousand rebel troops doing garrison duty in the city.

The nearest Union troops are at Fort Pulaski,

at the mouth of the river. They are in such close proximity to the rebel forces that if we could but escape the vigilance of our guard we should be almost certain of reaching the Federal lines in safety.

KIND TREATMENT AT SAVANNAH.

So great is the contrast between our treatment here and at other places that we cannot but feel that fortune has certainly smiled kindly upon us for once.

Our camp contains several acres of land. There is a number of live oak trees, which will furnish a splendid shade during the oppressive heat of noon day.

This is truly the oasis in the desert of my prison life. The authorities have issued tents and cooking utensils to us, and seem inclined to alleviate suffering as far as lies within their power. We have pitched our tents in regular order, so that the camp has quite a military appearance.

Our senior officer, Col. Miller of New York, acts as commandant of the interior, and all requests and complaints are made through him to the rebel authorities. He also superintends the issuing of rations and policing of the camp. It is fortunate for us that our guard, the 1st Ga. Volunteers, have been prisoners of war, and have learned what we had a right to expect, from the magnanimous treatment they themselves have received from the Federal government. And then nature is kind to us, we are enabled to bear our sufferings more cheerfully than at first. Scenes which at home would chill the blood and destroy all peace of mind, have become so commonplace with us that we look upon them unmoved; 'tis a dangerous experiment to place one constantly amidst the misery and sufferings of others with no power to alleviate them.

A COMPARISON OF REBEL PRISONS.

At Richmond, Danville and Macon, the authorities adopted a course, which they believed would forever render us unfit for further military duty. Their means were starvation, close confinement in filthy dungeons, and cruel treatment. The slightest pretext was sufficient to increase its severity. Evidently at Savannah, they have not yet learned the usual method of ridding the Confederacy of its enemies.

There are many rumors in circulation to-day, concerning Gen. Stoneman's raid; it is rumored that he is marching on Macon and Andersonville.

It is also reported, that the first six hundred prisoners sent from Macon, attempted to disarm the guard and take the train between this place and Charleston. The attempt seems to have proved a failure, as the guard had assistance from some temporary troops stationed along the rail road.

The faintest ray of hope seemed sufficient to cause an attempt to regain their freedom, although they knew full well the bitter results of an unsuccessful effort.

BETTER RATIONS.

Aug. 22. Our rations, though barely sufficient to sustain what little vitality we have left, are of a better quality than we have received before, since our capture.

The following is our daily allowance: Corn meal, one pint; fresh beef, one pound; rice, one gill; salt, one ounce for four days.

Sutlers are allowed to sell to us in camp; but having been robbed of our money, and nearly all our valuables when captured, we are generally very poor customers. We gradually find ourselves dispossessed of whatever remains to us of value, such as rings, lockets, etc., which we succeeded in concealing from our captors.

These souvenirs of the past were disposed of to purchase the necessaries of life, which we could have at the following prices: Flour, four dollars per quart; onions, three for a dollar; potatoes, forty-eight dollars per bushel; bread, two dollars per loaf; butter, ten dollars per pound; eggs, six dollars per dozen; apples, three for a dollar; milk, three dollars per quart.

At such prices we, of course, soon wasted away what we chanced to have; and this done, these land sharks ceased their visits, and we had to again content ourselves with what the rebel government saw fit to furnish.

BRICK OVENS.

The authorities have been kind enough to make an issue of brick, with which to build ovens. We raise them about two feet from the ground. The brick are arranged in an oval form, and strongly cemented together with mortar made of clay, which is very adhesive, and serves as a good substitute for lime and mortar.

We use these ovens principally for baking our corn bread, which is prepared by stirring the meal and cold water together. When baked, this bread is as heavy, and almost as hard as the iron skillet in which it is baked. Still, it is far preferable to that produced by the usual method of cooking.

TUNNELING.

Tunneling, as a means of escape, has become quite an institution.

A tunnel was commenced some days ago from a well, which we had dug and abandoned for this purpose. None but the working party were in the secret; and they themselves sworn not to divulge our plans.

Tools were frequently brought in for cleaning the camp, and we managed to keep some of these generally for a day or two, until a search was instituted for them, when they were left exposed in some other part of the camp for the rebels to find.

OUR SCHEME EXPOSED BY A COW.

The tunnel was soon finished, and it had been carried several feet outside of the stockade line, when, to the great surprise of the parties interested, upon opening it, found that another chain of sentinels was placed some twenty feet from the stockade. When this discovery was made we carefully concealed the opening, resolving to carry it beyond the second line of sentinels the next night; but, unfortunately for us, before night came, a cow, passing over the tunnel, broke through. The rebels, seeing the unpleasant situation of the unfortunate creature, went to her assistance, and were thus enabled to discover our intentions.

.The tunnel was filled up, the camp carefully inspected, and the most severe penalties attached to another attempt to escape.

JOY WITHOUT, DEATH WITHIN THE STOCKADE.

Aug. 26. This has been a gala day for the rebels at this point. A picnic has been given to the rebel troops stationed here by the ladies of Savannah. It was held a short distance from our camp — so near that our ears have been greeted by lively music, joyous peals of laughter, and happy voices.

How many sacred memories of other days did this scene recall. Freedom certainly seemed a precious gift to them. It will be doubly so to us if we are ever permitted to regain it; and hence, in the future, we may be compensated for our present loss. But to many of us the day has been as sad within the stockade as seemingly joyous without.

One of our number, Capt. McGinnis, died this morning. He had a large number of friends among the prisoners, and was held in high esteem for his many noble qualities; but the severity of prison life had done its work, and he was gone; and we were desirous that one so brave and noble as he had proved himself to be should have, at least, a decent burial. Therefore we appointed a committee to wait upon the commandant of the camp, Col. Wayne, to request that we be permitted to give the captain a decent burial; but received from him the response that the captain was

"NOTHING BUT A DAMNED YANKEE,"

deserving to be buried like a dog, and so he should be. We needed not even this reply to teach us how perfectly heartless was the man; for nature had written the lines of baseness on his face. His eyes constantly betrayed the utter immorality of his heart, and branded him "villain;" but, fortunately for us, he was an exception to the officers of his command, who were ever courteous and obliging, as far as lay within their power.

KINDNESS OF LADIES.

We were greatly surprised this evening upon receiving a note from the ladies of the town, informing us that they had learned with pain of Col. Wayne's answer to our petition, and that they themselves have purchased a burial lot unbeknown to the colonel, where the captain's remains will be suitably interred under their direction. Thank God for this dear womanly act!

Aug. 30. An exchange of army chaplains and surgeons has been effected; and those held as prisoners at this point are to take passage north on the next flag of truce boat, and will leave this place for Charleston on the 4 o'clock P. M. train.

The wildest enthusiasm prevails among them. An exchange from close confinement, in the hands of an enemy, to perfect freedom among ones friends is certainly a sufficient cause for exultation and joy.

The D.D.s and M.D.s are now the great centre of attraction with the prisoners. Crowds have been collecting around them all day, with some message for their friends at home, which they promise sacredly to deliver.

They will be sadly missed by us; for they were untiring in their labors while here.

Aug. 31. Weather warm and sultry. Played chess this afternoon with Lieut. Apple, 1st Md. Cavalry.

Sept. 1. We have heard heavy canonading in the direction of Charleston since morning, which is doubtless owing to the philosophical fact that damp atmosphere is a good conductor of sound.

Sept. 2. Washed my underclothing in the morning. Played chess in the afternoon with Lieut. Wadsworth, 16th Me.

Sept. 3. The heat was very oppressive during the day. Called on friend Hampton, and was surprised to find him quite low with chronic rheumatism. He will be admitted to the hospital to-morrow.

Sept. 4. Made the acquaintance of Lieut. Merry, of the 106th N. Y. Infantry, formerly of Ogdensburgh. Had a very pleasant chat with M., he is acquainted with many of my old friends in St. Lawrence Co.

Sept. 11. Exchange stock above par to-day.

It is rumored that we are to be sent to Charleston in the morning for exchange, but few however, are inclined to invest, as it is more than probable that if removed at all, we shall be taken to the besieged city to share the fate of our fellow officers who were sent thither from Macon.

CHAPTER VII.

IN CHARLESTON JAIL YARD.

"Oh thou doomed city of the evil seed,
  Long nursed by baneful passion's heated breath;
Now bursts the germ, and lo, the evil deed
  Invites the sword of war the stroke of death."

September 12, 1864. We were marched out of Camp Davidson by our old guard at six o'clock, A. M., for this place, and I could say with Byron's Prisoner of Chilon, "even I left my prison walls with a sigh," but from far different reasons, for at Savannah we were treated with some of the respect that we are entitled to as prisoners of war, and now we were destined for Charleston, to be placed under the fire of our own batteries, for the enemy seem to think that we may be the means of saving the besieged city from the doom which inevitably awaits it. Of course they affirm that this is retaliation, but with the north retaliation has ever been looked upon as a sad extremity, and to be exercised only when no other resource remains for restraining the excesses of its foes. With the rebels, the slightest pretext has been sufficient to cause the most wanton destruction of life.

After leaving our camp at Savannah, we were turned over to the City Battallion which guarded us through town.

We remained for a number of hours in the dusty streets of the city, under the scorching heat of the sun, when we were ordered into cattle cars, weary and sick at heart, yet not entirely despondent, for there is

> "No grief so great, but runneth to an end,
> No hap so hard, but will in time amend."

One of our number was permitted by some of the guard to step out of his car at the first station, but was immediately fired upon by several others.

The prisoner only saved himself by dodging under a car and remaining there until the excitement was over, when he was dragged from his hiding place and thrown back among his fellows.

And yet these men who could thus murderously fire upon a defenceless prisoner guilty of no offence, were constantly talking of their honor and their chivalry. Well, let them babble, the record of their acts will live longer than their words.

We reached this city in the afternoon, and were marched down Coming street to our present quarters in Charleston Jail Yard.

Sept. 16. The jail yard is situated in the south east portion of the city, and in plain view of Morris Island, on which our batteries are planted, which have done such fearful execution. It is in the most filthy condition conceivable, having been occupied for a long time by prisoners and convicts, without ever having been cleaned. We are unable to obtain even the necessary tools from the authorities, to do this work ourselves. Its sanitary condition is such, that it seems impossible for us to remain here long without suffering from some foul and malignant disease.

We are without shelter. Fragments of tents are still standing, but have ceased to afford any protection from the sun or storm, for the prisoners who were confined here before us, many of whom were from Andersonville, were in such a destitute condition upon their arrival, that they cut the tents to pieces to make themselves clothes to wear.

What is commonly called the "Burnt District" is between the jail yard and Morris Island; it covers about one-third of the city. It was burnt during the early part of the year, having been set on fire by the explosion of shell thrown from our batteries.

This part of the city has been deserted by all except the negroes, who, whenever there is a cessation of shelling for a short time, flock here in great numbers to save rent. But a few shell dropped into the streets will soon disperse them, although they are easily tempted back again. And after a few days of quiet, they may be seen trudging around with bundles on their backs, looking for the most favorable location, often taking up their quarters in the dwellings of the former notables. Before the siege the poor negroes could only gain admission by the back entrance, where with hat in hand they awaited the orders of "Massa."

Well, truth is stranger than fiction, and the city built by the hard labor of slaves, now holds them as her principal occupants.

Sixty shell and solid shot of very heavy calibre were thrown into the city to-day, many of which exploded very near the yard. Fragments from two struck between this enclosure and the Marine Hospital, in which a large number of prisoners are confined. The explosion of nearly every shell thrown by our batteries may be seen by us.

The prisoners constantly wear a forlorn and haggard look, owing in a great measure to starvation and exposure to danger, even one who has been in many engagements knows but little of the effects of our situation. I have noticed on the battle field, that the most critical time for the army, when there is the greatest danger of confusion and disorder generally followed by a panic, is when the men are exposed to a heavy artillery fire, and are not actively engaged themselves; they must have something to do to occupy the attention. Now conceive of men placed constantly under fire day and night for months, with nothing but their own sad fate to occupy their minds, and is it strange that many have become hopelessly insane, while others have been incapacitated for all the duties of life hereafter, nothing but strong nerves and an inflexible will can save one under such circumstances.

Sept. 18. A large number of shell have exploded very near our yard to-day, but we have escaped unharmed.

CHARLESTON JAIL AND ITS INMATES.

Charleston Jail, near which we are confined, is filled with prisoners, many of whom are negro soldiers captured during our assault on Fort Wagner. There are also a large number of southern convicts confined in the same building, as well as several officers and soldiers of the rebel army, guilty of military offences.

I had a conversation with Sergt. Johnson (colored), Co. F, 55th Regt. Mass. Infantry; he was a full blooded negro, but possessed of no ordinary degree of intelligence, he gave me an interesting history of the captivity and trial of the negro prisoners. Soon after their capture they were informed, that they were to be tried by a civil commission on a charge of having abandoned their masters and enlisted in the United States army, and if found guilty, they were told that they might make up their minds to stretch hemp. And why should they not be found guilty? to be sure, nearly all were from the north and had always been free; but they knew full well, that this court was formed, not to subserve the ends of justice, but to convict, for the rebels had sufficiently illustrated their method of dealing with negro prisoners, that is, when they deigned to receive them as such, instead of murdering them in cold blood, in order to convince their comrades of the narrow chances for life, should they unfortunately fall into the hands of an enemy.

A FRIEND.

Sergeant J. told me that they were surprised to find a friend in a relative of Ex-Gov. Pickens, who, although a resident of Charleston, and educated under her institutions, yet had tendered his services unrecompensed to them.

INCLINED TO BE DISTRUSTFUL.

The sergeant related that when he first came among them, and revealed his intention to act in their behalf, he was regarded as an imposter, a government detective, whose only object was to learn their history; that is, to ascertain if they had been slaves, to whom they had belonged, and under what circumstances they had left their masters.

AN ACT OF TRUE NOBLENESS.

He gave them money to buy little necessaries (for nothing but corn meal was issued to them, and this in very small quantities), and left them with the promise that he would soon return, and report the progress of his investigations; but when he came, he found them still doubting, and unwilling to place confidence in him; but, calling them together, he related that before the war he himself was a slaveholder, and was known and respected throughout his state. But at the commencement of this intestine strife, having proved true to the old flag, his property had been swept from him, his friends had deserted him, calling him traitor, and an abolitionist, and that now he was an outcast among his friends, and in constant danger of being assassinated.

GENUINE PATRIOTISM.

He also told them that he knew that this must be his fate, from the first, if he remained true to his convictions; but that, having counted the cost, it was as nothing when weighed in the balance against truth; and he was now prepared to do his work thoroughly and unhesitatingly, regarding only as friends those who were true to the cause of their country.

By this means he gained their confidence; for there is

A HIGHER LANGUAGE THAN THE WRITTEN.

'Tis seen in the mute dropping of the tear, in the trembling of the lip, in the flashing of the eye, in the glory and grandeur that speaks at times through the very tenement of the soul. 'Tis the court of appeals, from which there can be no appeal.

We listen to the words of a man, and then we look into his eyes to interpret his meaning; and this decision cannot be revoked. And when this language shall become as universally studied and understood as the written language which we speak, then shall the divine command "Thou shalt not lie," never be violated on account of the inability of mankind to deceive us with their words.

As the sergeant related to me how untiring were the efforts of this friend during their prolonged and doubtful trial in combating truth against error, in proving their innocence, even under laws that were made but for white men, he seemed at times to be completely overcome by his feelings, so unused was he to sympathy or kind words; but when their trial was once over, and their innocence established, they returned to jail, to be regarded as prisoners of war.

THE LAST VISIT.

It was after their return to the jail that their friend and advocate visited them for the last time. Their emotions were uncontrollable, and they seemed unable to give even a faint expression of their gratitude, to him who had sacrificed so much for them. Their admiration for this devoted friend of the Union is so great, that the mere mention of his name is sufficient to bring tears to the eyes of these swarthy sons, who have thus far, had so little to be grateful to *us* for.

The convicts and negro prisoners are granted the limits of the yard. They frequently rehearse their sufferings to us. In the evening the colored prisoners often gather around the jail, and sing their plaintive melodies till late in the evening. The character of their songs is usually mournful; and it is often affecting to listen to them — always embodying, as they do, those simple, child-like emotions and sentiments for which the negro is so justly celebrated.

The harmony and rich melody of their voices are rarely surpassed. Indeed, this seems a special gift to them.

One song, which appeared to be a special favorite with them, was written by Sergeant Johnson, whom I have before mentioned. He intended it as a parody on "*This Cruel War.*" I give the song as he furnished it to me.

I.

"When I enlisted in the army,
  Then I thought 'twas grand,
Marching through the streets of Boston
  Behind a regimental band.
When at Wagner I was captured,
  Then my courage failed;
Now I'm lousy, hungry, naked,
  Here in Charleston jail.

CHORUS. Weeping, sad and lonely —
    Oh! how bad I feel;
  Down in Charleston, South Carolina,
    Praying for a good "square meal."

II.

If Jeff. Davis will release me,
  Oh, how glad I'll be;
When I get on Morris Island,
  Then I shall be free.
Then I'll tell those conscript soldiers
  How they use us here;
Giving us an old "corn dodger"—
  They call it prisoner's fare.

III.

We are longing, watching, praying,
  But will not repine,
Till Jeff. Davis does release us,
  And sends us "in our lines."

> Then with words of kind affection,
>   How they'll greet us there!
> Wondering how we could live so long
>   Upon the "dodger's fare."
> CHORUS. Then we will laugh long and loudly —
>   Oh, how glad we'll feel,
> When we arrive on Morris Island
>   And eat a good "square meal."

The negroes sang this song with a great deal of zest, as it related to their present sufferings, and was just mournful enough to excite our sympathy. A large number of the prisoners now confined with us were removed here from Andersonville; and I have listened with disgust and perfect horror to the history of their past treatment. Future generations will stand aghast in view of the unheard of and pitiless deeds of men, steeped in infamy — their foul and barbarous usage of our unfortunate soldiers.

At Andersonville large numbers were crowded into a small space, where the ground was literally alive with vermin. During the heat of day, by watching closely in the warm sand, you could perceive a constant motion among the particles; so alive was it with lice. On such ground as this, the men were closely crowded together, without shelter, and with fare which a rebel surgeon himself declared "would produce disease among swine."

AWFUL CONDITION OF THE HOSPITAL.

The hospital was in the most wretched condition; no one left the pen however feeble he might be, who had any friend to attend to his wants, for the only advantage gained by leaving the stockade, was a shelter from the scorching rays of the sun, but this was counterbalanced by being brought in such immediate contact with so many afflicted with the most foul and offensive diseases.

GREAT SUFFERING.

The men were placed upon the ground, nothing underneath them, and usually without covering, while the nights were so chilling, as to keep the poor fellows quaking with cold until the sun appeared again to warm them, and then followed the other extreme, the intense heat, which rendered the sufferings of those intolerable, whose blood was almost quenched with burning fevers.

The rebel surgeons seemed to give them little or no care.

LIVING DEATH.

So filthy and obnoxious, so infested with vermin, and so loathsome had this den of living death become, that it was indeed impossible for a person of good health to endure it long.

While such a state of things existed, it is not strange that the mortality among them was fearful. Each day the dead were carried away by scores, their places to be again filled by others, who in all probability would soon share the same fate, for none but those who were so low as to be past cure were ever looked at by the surgeons, and nearly as many died within the pen, without ever receiving any medical treatment, as in the hospital.

A fearful responsibility certainly rests somewhere, and men who could thus wantonly murder so many helpless and innocent men, are almost as much to be pitied for their moral depravity as the prisoners for their bodily suffering, and yet these martyrs to the cause of "Liberty and their Country," never murmured against the government, always believing that it was powerless to help them, or else that it did not understand their true condition.

I have noticed scarcely a prisoner from Andersonville, who was not more or less affected by some disease contracted there, so that we now see the truthfulness of what they say proven by their physical condition.

A THUNDER STORM.

Sept. 20. I find myself weak and exhausted this morning, with blood feverish and my system racked with pain, the result of yesterday's suffering; for it was one of the most wretched days that I have passed since my captivity.

Nothing could have been more lovely than the morning, but the sky was soon overcast with dark clouds, and one of the most fearful thunder storms broke forth that I have ever witnessed, followed by a severe and drenching rain, which continued during the day and night.

REFUSED ADMISSION TO THE JAIL.

We were without shelter, or wood to build fires, and were obliged to exercise constantly to keep from chilling. At night, as there were no signs of the storm abating, we sent a committee to wait upon the jailor, to obtain permission if possible, to go inside the jail, as there were a number of unoccupied cells, but were refused admission without a reason being given.

Before morning the yard became flooded with water some four or five inches deep, and, with our garments drenched and our limbs benumbed with cold, we were compelled to walk through this flood, in order to keep up a circulation of the blood.

There were a few small out buildings connected with the jail, formerly used as sinks, and which were in the most loathsome and filthy condition; yet into these a small portion of the prisoners crowded themselves, and were partially protected from the storm, but suffered almost as severely from the obnoxious vapors, as we from the drenching rain.

A CONTRAST.

I have frequently read of the effect produced upon persons by living upon a shelf of rocks, or on a barren sand tract, or perhaps in pleasant valleys, surrounded by grand and soul inspiring mountains, and have wondered if the influences in the outer world were so potent for good or evil, what must be the effect upon us, whose vision cannot extend beyond the dismal walls which surround this abode of misery. The monotony too, is only relieved by a "jail," a "work house," and the whizzing, bursting shell.

SHELLS A SUBJECT FOR DISCUSSION.

Many are the discussions, many the dissertations upon the subject of shells.

Some for an argument claim, that a shell in its progress through the air is entirely harmless if it does not explode before reaching a point directly overhead; while others assert, that a shell must necessarily reach an angle of at least 48 degrees, in order to secure perfect safety to a person directly beneath.

Groups of officers collect from time to time, some, around the old wooden pump, which serves as a stand for the speaker—others beneath the shade of an old fig tree which stands in one corner of the yard, for the purpose of mutually benefitting themselves by arguments upon this, and various other subjects.

Hours are spent thus, whilst every fifteen or twenty minutes we could see the smoke and hear the explosion of "Foster's messengers," as we call them, which come to us in the shape of screeching, tearing, death dealing, two-hundred pound shells; and, although we are completely isolated from the outer world, yet these "terrible dispatches" seem ever welcome. They tell us of the untiring perseverance of our forces on Morris Island.

So correct is their aim, so well do the gunners know of our whereabouts, that shells burst all around in front, and often fly screeching directly over head without injury to us.

When the distant rumbling of the "Swamp angel" is heard, and the cry "here it comes!" resounds through the yard, slumberers, the drowsy, the thoughtful souls, in fact all start, endeavoring to see where the messenger will fall. Perhaps it will burst in mid air; perhaps fall, crashing through the roof of some dwelling, which will not remain standing long after the explosion.

It is a singularly noticeable *fact*, that every Charleston paper, in its report of "damage done the city" by our batteries, never chronicles the loss of a white person; but in every morning edition we notice the name of some "poor negro," whose life has been taken by the "cruel barbarity of the d—d Yankees."

The sight at night is truly beautiful. We trace along the sky a slight stream of fire, similar to the tail of a comet; follow its course until, "*whiz, whiz,*" come the little pieces from our mighty 200-pounders, like "grape shot," scattering themselves all around, and telling us, in unmistakable language, that our soldiers are still battling for the cause of freedom inviolate.

Sept. 22. Heat oppressive. Heard from the members of my regiment, who are confined in Roper Hospital. They are making an effort to have R. and myself transferred to that building, which is a far better place than the jail yard, although it is quite as much exposed to shot and shell.

Sept. 23. The naval officers are in excellent spirits at present, having learned by the last flag of truce boat, that terms for a special exchange of all naval prisoners have been agreed upon.

Sept. 24. Sixty shell have been thrown into the city to-day.

Two hundred prisoners transferred to Roper and Marine hospitals.

Sept. 25. Shelling kept up vigorously during the past forty-eight hours. Many explosions very near us. No casualties among the prisoners.

Sept. 26. Met friend H. to-day, one of the naval officers, who expects to be included on the list for special exchange next week. If so, he assures me that I shall have his shirt, as he can dispense with under clothing until he reaches our lines, where he is sure of doing decidedly better. He will also bear a message to my friends in Troy. Eighty shell have been thrown into town since yesterday.

ROPER HOSPITAL.

Sept. 29. To-day is an eventful one for R. and myself. Our rations being entirely gone, we started in quest of something to eat, after taking our usual morning wash. We succeeded in finding a friend who had a little corn meal left, and who willingly shared it with us.

Hastening back to our quarters, we converted it into mush, and sat down fully prepared to do ample justice to the dish, when a cry was heard, "All those whose names are called will prepare to go to Roper Hospital immediately."

We listen, but our names are not called; we wait and wait for the next list to be read. It seems evident that we are destined to remain in the jail yard, when, to our great surprise, we hear the welcome voice of Maj. E. F. Cooke, of the old regiment, who has at last succeeded in persuading the authorities to remove us from this hell on earth. How we start! How eagerly do we grasp his extended hand! He tells us to "pack up," which requires but a moment, as our wardrobe is very scanty, and our equipments few. Passing through the heavy doors of the jail, it seems as though a new life had sprung up within us. We feel free, although the rebel bayonets still surround us. We are taken before the commandant, to whom we give our paroles not to attempt an escape; and are then passed through the gateway of "Roper" into the beautiful garden of the hospital. On our right is a palmetto, on our left an orange tree, while around us bloom flowers of every hue, whose very fragrance inspires us with new life. How great the change. Here we are comparatively free. Here all seem better contented. We are assigned quarters on the third floor *piazza;* the hard floor seeming a luxury, and the place itself a paradise, compared to that worse than grave — Charleston Jail Yard.

SISTERS OF CHARITY.

Confined as we are, so far away from every home comfort and influence, from all that makes life worth living for, how quickly do we notice the first kind word, the passing friendly glance.

Can any prisoner, confined here, ever forget the "Sisters of Charity?" Ask the poor private, now suffering in those loathsome hospitals, so near us, if he *can* forget the kind look, the kind word given him by that "Sister," while burning with fever, or racked with pain? Many are the bunches of grapes, many the sip of its pure juice, does the sufferer get from her hands. They seem — they are *ministering angels*; and while all around us are *our avowed enemies*, they remain true to every instinct of womanhood. They *dare* lift the finger to help, they *do* relieve many a sufferer.

See them moving in our midst, known by their peculiar dress. They are reverenced. We shake them heartily by the hand, and, as we follow them in their course through our rooms, we feel, as the poet has written —

> "Woman! Blest partner of our joys and woes!
> Even in the darkest hour of earthly ill,
> Untarnished yet, thy fond affection glows,
> Throbs with each pulse, and beats with every thrill!
> Bright o'er the wasted scene thou hoverest still,
> Angel of comfort to the failing soul;
> Undaunted by the tempest wild and chill
> That pours its restless and disastrous roll,

> O'er all that blooms below, with sad and hollow howl.
> When sorrow rends the heart, when feverish pain
> Wrings the hot drops of anguish from the brow,
> To soothe the soul, to cool the burning brain,
> O! who so welcome, and so prompt as thou!
> The battle's hurried scene, and angry glow,
> The death-encircled pillow of distress,
> The lonely moments of secluded woe—
> Alike thy care and constancy confess,
> Alike thy pitying hand and fearless friendship bless."

Were other denominations in the south as active in aiding us as the Catholics have been, I might have some faith in rebel Christianity.

Sept. 30. Several shell passed directly over us this afternoon, a fragment of one striking the west end of the building.

Oct. 1. Yellow fever is raging fearfully in the city at present. Five shell from our batteries fell in the burnt district to-day. It was amusing to witness the flocks of negroes, who came running from the buildings which they have occupied since the commencement of the siege clear of rent charges, the owners being too timid to remain in that locality. The colored people are often driven out in this manner, but invariably return after the shelling, to enjoy their threatened haunts.

Oct. 5. The rebel captain commanding this prison, and also his adjutant, died last night with yellow fever. Many prisoners have been swept off by the same, during the past four days. We heard from our enlisted men at Charleston Race Course to-day. Starvation, exposure and the frightful ravages of yellow fever, are sweeping them off by the score.

CHAPTER VIII.

REMOVAL TO COLUMBIA, S. C., CAMP SORGHUM.*

At eight o'clock on the morning of the fifth of October we left Charleston, S. C., where we had been confined for six weeks, for the most part within the enclosure of the jail yard, securely packed in cattle cars, and guarded by the 32d Regiment Georgia volunteers, to whom too much credit cannot be given. The kind treatment bestowed upon us by the officers and men of this splendid regiment was more than we had ever received at the hands of our captors. Our journey was marked with no features of peculiar interest, as the country through which we passed was a barren and sandy tract, with no vegetation to meet the weary eye, save occasionally a small patch of cotton, and sometimes sugar cane growing by the roadside.

* So named, because that was the principal ration issued while there.

REBEL VIGILANCE.

The change of base occupied about fourteen hours, when we arrived at Columbia, in the midst of a terrific rain storm, without food, blankets, or a necessary amount of clothing. We were compelled to vacate our quarters in the cars, and take up with such as were provided us by the Confederate officers in command, to wit: none at all.

We were closely guarded, and a lieutenant, whose name I do not recollect, received a serious wound in the back by a bayonet in the hands of one of the sentinels, for attempting to take a small loaf of bread offered him by a sympathizing citizen.

We remained in an open field on "Bridge street," during the night, suffering from hunger, without blankets, tents, or any conveniences for comfort, at the mercy of the elements, with four pieces of artillery trained upon the ground which we occupied.

PEACE MOVEMENTS.

The rebels commented much upon the course pursued by Mr. Stephens, their vice president, regarding peace movements, and expressed great anxiety for a knowledge of the result; wishing for peace, they hope the movement may terminate in a settlement of our difficulties, upon a basis satisfactory to the interests of the southern people.

Thus passed our first night at

COLUMBIA.

The capital city of the first state in the grand unity of states, to raise the dark hand of treason and adopt the base acts of secession, which hurled the hosts of America, who had for upwards of eighty years enjoyed all the quietness of peace, into the fierce havoc and chaos of war, making our own beautiful land run red with the blood of her noble sons.

This city is one of the finest in the state, has a population of about 20,000 souls, is handsomely situated on a gentle rise of ground, overlooking the surrounding country in all directions for a distance of from twenty to thirty miles, and is on the line of the South Carolina Central Rail Road, equi-distant from Charleston and Wilmington, N. C.

It is also on the north bank of the Congaree river, and 125 miles from the sea.

It is regularly laid out, its streets crossing each other at right angles; some are wide and planted with handsome trees, among which are found the Palmetto which is familiar to all, as it was represented upon the first flag raised as a signal of war in opposition to the laws of our country.

Except in the busy, commercial parts of the town, the houses are surrounded with gardens, crowded with shrubs and flowers of all kinds; each establishment being generally encircled with hedges of hawthorn, interspersed with a luxuriant growth of roses.

The houses, which stand amid these beautiful pleasure grounds, are built of many different forms. Those of wood are usually painted white.

To the southerner, this lovely place, during the war, has been one of perfect safety.

It being the farthest of any from the lines of our advancing armies, and free from attack by our ever watchful navy; many have flocked here from all parts of the Confederacy, where they might be beyond the reach of the dread sounds of war.

The Confederate government, influenced by the thought of impending danger, moved its treasury from the city of Richmond to this place, fearing that the Union army might make an inroad into its capital, and destroy its worthless currency.

The public buildings are of magnificent structure.

The Capitol, or State House, occupies a commanding position near the centre of the town.

The grounds adjoining are adorned with beautiful walks and avenues.

The Military Academy, Court House, and its church edifices are built in splendid style.

With all the beauty and magnificence combined to make these buildings grand to look upon, there yet remains connected with their history the memory of the dark deeds perpetrated within their walls, which resulted in the dismemberment of the Palmetto state from our great and glorious Union.

Here it was that the first steps were taken, which placed South Carolina foremost in the ranks of those states which afterwards adopted the ordinance of secession.

Although coöperation had been urged by many leading men of the south, among whom were Mr. Rhett, long conspicuous in the councils of the state, and Mr. Trenholm, afterwards a member of the Confederate cabinet, yet the fiery devotees of slavery forced their opinions, and controlled the public feeling until a convention was called, which met on the 20th of December, 1860, when South Carolina launched forth upon a sea, above whose tranquil bosom brooded a pent up storm, dark and tremendous, which, when it burst forth from its deathly silence, carried all away who had embarked upon its alluring surface, and dashing in one final wreck the frail structure, upon which this unrighteous and unjust government was to be formed.

She entered upon a struggle which has devastated her lovely fields and finest cities, depopulated many of her most flourishing towns, and reduced her inhabitants to poverty, degradation and despair.

By this deed, thousands of America's honored sons, while battling nobly for the maintenance of right, have been sacrificed—making the fields of the south run red with blood.

But it has terminated in the complete overthrow of the foundation upon which these southern leaders attempted to rear their government, and in the destruction of that evil which had so long stained our nation's honor. Oh! Columbia, the pride of the south, thou hast passed through the fierce and bloody struggle without sharing in the general ruin which follows the footsteps of war. Although many of your hearth-stones have been made desolate, your beauty and magnificence yet remain.

May your people profit by the sad lot of other cities, and no more sacrifice their honor by raising the fierce and bloody hand of treason in opposition to their country.*

MORNING AFTER THE STORM.

Oct. 7. The storm had abated. The clouds broke away, and once more the sun arose in splendor, shedding its refulgent light upon the fair city, and upon the weary, wretched band of unfortunates who had clustered together during the past dark and stormy night, in a strange land, far from home, family and friends, with everything possible added to our wretched condition by our brutal keepers to make us more miserable.

TURNED OUT TO GRASS.

Corn meal and sorghum were issued to us in small quantities, and then we were moved from our camp on Bridge street to the south side of the Congaree, about two miles from the city,

* This chapter was written since the escape.

and, like Nebuchadnezzar of old, turned out to grass.

An attempt was made yesterday by the authorities to persuade us to take our paroles, in order that we might enjoy the privileges of an open field. We were threatened with confinement in some old tobacco houses in case we did not comply with their wishes; but we sternly refused to accept their base proposition, and utterly disregarded their threats, knowing that our condition could be made no worse by the change.

For some reason unbeknown to us, we were not removed from this place into the tobacco houses; but a guard and dead line were established; and in the open field, with no covering save the broad canopy of heaven, our band, numbering upwards of fifteen hundred men, was obliged to remain.

Many of our number, worn out by the confinement of prison life, with nature exhausted by exposure to the weather, and for want of nourishment, yielded up their spirits to the God who gave them, and were buried in the southern land by the hands of their enemies, with no stone to mark their final resting place.

> "Hallow ye, each lonely grave,
>   Make their memory sure and blest,
> For their lives they nobly gave,
>   And their spirits are at rest."

NEWS FROM THE ARMY.

After many unsuccessful attempts to get a newspaper, I at last, by bribing one of our guards, secured a copy of the *South Carolinian*—a weekly sheet, published in the city—from which I learned the position of the Union army under the gallant Sherman.

A DAY OF JOY.

Oct. 8. This day was one of joy and thanksgiving. Our hearts were made glad, and our hopes brighter, by the receipt of clothing, and many other articles of comfort sent to us from the north by that ever beneficent organization, the Sanitary Commission.

Those of our number who were the most needy were supplied with such articles as the authorities saw fit to allow them, which to some degree alleviated their sufferings, and made life somewhat sweeter.

It was my happy lot to get a towel and an undershirt.

The last mentioned article was of great value to me, as more than three months had passed since I had had a change.

Notwithstanding the distribution of clothing, many were without shoes, stockings, shirts and coats—dying by inches for want of some protection from the inclement weather. They submitted to their fate, however, trusting in the government and the ability of their country to save them before they finally perished.

> "Hope comes again to the heart, long a stranger;
> Once more she sings me her flattering strain;
> But hush, gentle siren, for ah! there's less danger
> In still suffering on than in hoping again."

VOTING UPON THE PRESIDENTIAL CANDIDATES.

Oct. 16. Our prison pen had been remarkably quiet for six or eight days; nothing having transpired among the prisoners to cause any excitement; and we were fast falling into a state of melancholy sadness, when, in view of the approaching presidential election, it was suggested that we vote upon the subject ourselves. The idea was approved by most of our number, as it was also by the rebels; for they wished to get an expression of the prevailing sentiment among us, that they might the better judge of the feeling which pervaded the people at the north. By our action they could form some idea in reference to the intentions of our government and its supporters, there being among us men from every loyal state in the Union. Accordingly, notice was duly given to all who wished to make manifest their preference in the candidates for the presidency to meet at the quarters of the senior officer from their respective states, and vote for their declared favorite.

THE TEST AND ITS RESULT.

Much discussion as to the relative merits of the opposing candidates followed, and all awaited with anxiety the counting of the ballots.

I cast my vote for Abraham Lincoln, as did my messmates, Lieuts. Hampton and Richardson;. deeply regretting that it was my sad lot to be denied the privilege of doing so where it might count for some good. At six o'clock P. M. the counting was finished; the result being 1,024 votes for Lincoln, and 143 for McClellan.

This was the expression of feeling and opinion among men who had been deprived of all the common comforts of life, half starved, with nothing but dirty rags hanging to their emaciated limbs to protect their bodies from the cold, wasting away by hunger and exposure, yet would not favor a peace degrading to their country's honor.

Cheer upon cheer arose from our feeble voices, and resounded through our prison yard, upon the announcement, making the McClellanites, who had been very confident of the success of their candidate, look crest-fallen and disappointed.

The Confederates understood the significance of the reëlection of Mr. Lincoln full well.

They knew it would be impossible to free themselves from the serpent, into whose coils they had allowed themselves to be drawn; but that they must fight for a cause that originated in sin, which was nurtured in iniquity, unholy, unjust and hopeless.

The rebel officers had continually misrepresented the Federal administration to the prisoners; and as we had no means by which to refute the arguments of these wily secessionists, except the firm confidence in our government, our souls were filled with joy and gladness by this favorable result of our impromptu election.

"The song of war shall echo through the mountains
Till not one hateful link remains

Of slavery's lingering chains;
Till not one tyrant treads our plains,
Nor traitor lips pollute our fountains."

AN ESCAPE.

October 18. Our camp was thrown into a state of wild excitement, owing to the escape of three prisoners, who ran the guard and made towards "God's country." Several shots were fired at them as they passed the outer line, but without doing them any injury, and they passed out in safety. The entire guard was aroused. The men flew to arms—the artillerymen to their guns. The rebel officers, calling loudly to their men to fall in, could be distinctly heard at my quarters, making me tremble for the fate of the brave men who, risking life, were trying to make their escape from this den of misery. After the occurrence of this affair, our guard was redoubled, and orders given to the sentinels to shoot down every prisoner who should in any manner approach the "dead line." This action on the part of the Confederates did not, however, intimidate us in the least; for we well knew if compelled to remain there, in the condition we were then in, that death would surely overtake us; and to die in the attempt to free ourselves from the grasp of heartless tyrants would be no worse than starvation.

My plan for escape was not in the least disconcerted by this movement of the rebels; on the contrary, my determination to be free was more fixed in my mind, and I continued the preparations for a leave taking of Columbia, and the hated prison pen, "Camp Sorghum."

REJOICING OVER A SUCCESSFUL ESCAPE.

Oct. 20. Two more days passed, and no tidings were received from our friends who last escaped.

We were rejoicing over their safety, and had worked ourselves into a state of feverish excitement in consequence of their success in passing the "dead line," and were continually talking the matter over among ourselves.

When any of the prisoners freed themselves from the contaminating influences of this dreadful place, the remainder were not selfish, but held a jubilee, and prayed that it might be the good fortune of the escaped party to reach our lines in safety.

A PRISONER SHOT.

In the midst of our rejoicings the sad intelligence of the death of Lieut. George Young, of the 4th Regiment of Pa. Cavalry, was passed from mouth to ear until it reached me. I was overcome with grief at this report, for Lieut. Young was a brave man, a fine officer, a pleasant companion, and withal had been for a long time a suffering friend. He was shot in cold blood by one of the sentinels, while conversing with some fellow officers, near a small fire; he survived but a few moments.

Thus another noble spirit was ushered into the presence of its maker, sent thither by the brutal hand of a murderer.

Were they men and suffer such conduct? had they been taught the principles of love and justice, which are given to all in the great Book of Books? had they any sense of humanity in their bosoms? No, the foul fiend of darkness possessed and influenced their thoughts. Not satisfied with depriving men of the necessary food to sustain life, they shot down our defenceless comrades like dogs, without a shudder at the heinousness of the crime.

How long, oh God! how long will such fearful atrocities be allowed? From the time we left Charleston the weather had been exceedingly cold and disagreeable.

No tongue can tell or pen describe, the sufferings of the brave men confined here, the want of clothing made their bodies more susceptible of cold, and many were dying daily, by diseases brought on in consequence of exposure to the wind and storm, and the improper food furnished us under such circumstances.

THOUGHTS OF HOME.

It was customary with us to lay down after taking our night's meal, not to sleep, however, but to talk over the incidents of our boyhood days, and the events of our lives; when the thoughts of home and friends gathered around the fireside, would crowd themselves upon our minds, and not until the star of evening was dimmed by the light of approaching day, would we find that rest which our exhausted systems so much needed.

There were but few persons here who had ever been compelled to suffer such privations and hardships. Most of them before entering the army, had either been clerks behind the counter, a student in a lawyer's office, or a well-to-do mechanic, some were soldiers by profession; and many were sons of wealthy men, who had never known anything but pleasure, and had always taken life easy. But all through the common impulses of their natures and the patriotism ever burning in the loyal American heart, had offered their services to their bleeding and distracted country, to assist in subduing the element of discontent at the south, and the foulest and most unwarrantable rebellion against just and proper authority, ever known within the annals of time.

As to their fate, many were thoughtless and indifferent, some were distrustful of our government and its intentions to liberate them; but few were without hope of approaching succor, and depending upon the mercies of an allwise and overruling Providence, we made the best of our miserable condition.

I did not intend to remain in "durance vile" a great while longer; but upon the first favorable opportunity to take my flight, with some one or two of my friends, if they chose to go with me; if not, I should make the attempt alone.

I did not think any of my companions would refuse an offer to accompany me if I should propose a plan which presented any chances for success.

I kept my own counsels, however, and when the time should arrive, I would cautiously make my intentions known to those I wished to have accompany me, and then set out together. As the days came and went, our sufferings increased.

The season being far advanced, the cold night air chilled us through, and the stars, from their lofty stations in the heavens, shone upon us clear and cold, while the moon reflected its pale, silvery light upon our pallid faces, making us look doubly haggered and ghost-like.

ALLOWED TO GET WOOD BY TAKING A PAROLE.

Nov. 4. The prison authorities adopted a rule of allowing a certain number each day to pass outside the prison limits, for the purpose of backing in such quantities of wood as we could carry.

This privilege was granted to such as would give their paroles not to attempt an escape.

We were all very glad of the opportunity of doing something whereby the material could be procured for making a fire. Many accepted the offer, and went out to bring in what they could pick up in the shape of dry twigs, broken branches of trees and bark. It was a sad sight to see us filing along under guard, picking up what we could carry, and returning with our loads upon our backs.

Some of the men were so weak that they became as helpless as a child, and had to be carried back to camp in a state of utter exhaustion and insensibility. In trying to help themselves, they overtaxed their remaining strength, which brought on fevers and delirium, from the effects of which a large number died.

I profited, however, by the arrangement; for not only a sufficient quantity of wood was procured to last me and my mess two days, but in carefully examining the plan of our pen, and the system by which it was guarded, I obtained and added to my small store of knowledge much valuable information concerning the surrounding country. All of which, at some future day, then not far distant, would be put to good use.

I was not by any means the only one to profit by these explorations. Others, as much on the alert as myself for adventure, conceived plans whereby they effected an escape; but unfortunately, after a few days had passed, were generally re-captured and thrown into county jails.

They had the satisfaction, during their absence, of getting some corn bread and bacon of the faithful negroes, out of which they could make at least a few good meals; and never afterwards regretted that the attempt to get free had been made.

MY OLD SHOES.

My shoes being badly worn, I went to the "camp cobbler" to get them repaired. He gave me no encouragement, but said that they were past help, that they could not be mended.

How could I travel barefoot through the hot burning sand of the highway, the stone covered fields, or the dreary swamps? I must have some covering for my feet, and set about preparing something myself.

By dint of good luck, I obtained the rim of an old worn out regulation hat, from which I cut some inner soles for my old shoes, and by tying the outer sole to the uppers with a piece of cord, made them appear no worse, and added largely to their worth and durability; thus my feet were protected from the heat and cold, for a short time before my escape was effected.

TURNING NIGHT INTO DAY.

During the last two weeks of my stay at Columbia, the nights had become so cold that we did not think of lying down, but would walk around the camp for the purpose of keeping the blood in circulation and to prevent chilling.

When the sun arose in the east, then, and not till then, would we stretch ourselves upon the ground to sleep; the heat from its rays keeping us warm while locked in the arms of Morpheus.

A DAY OF ANXIETY.

Nov. 8. This eventful day was ushered in by us with great anxiety, as it was to decide who should be our chief magistrate for the next four years. We had but little uneasiness upon this subject, as we were satisfied that the election would result in placing Mr. Lincoln, our present worthy president, in the chair, which for the past four years he had filled with so much credit to himself, and honor to the nation.

DECEPTION PRACTICED BY THE PRISON AUTHORITIES.

We were also notified by the prison authorities, that a general exchange of prisoners would take place on the 20th. Capt. Hatch, the rebel commissioner of exchange was there, and it was rumored about camp, that a large portion of our number would be taken to Savannah immediately, causing great excitement.

The "fresh fish" especially were in excellent humor over what they styled glorious good news.

The old prisoners were not inclined however to be very jubilant over the announcement, as they had many times before been duped and deceived by the practical infamy of the Confederates. And it was very well that we put no faith in such loose reports, for at this time as on many other occasions when such rumors were circulated, nothing official had been received.

The rebels always took advantage of the natural despondency following so much excitement, to endeavor to persuade the prisoners to believe that their government cared nothing for their suffering, and would use every other means at their command to cause us to lose confidence in the Federal authorities and the commanding officers of our army. They miserably failed in their endeavors to extinguish the fire of patriotism burning in our bosoms, by such contemptible misrepresentations, and only added to the bitter hate in which we looked upon these vile traitors and inhuman wretches, who guarded and starved us.

CAUGHT BY HOUNDS.

Nov. 9. This has been a most beautiful day. Seventeen of the recently escaped prisoners were brought in this morning; forty-eight have now been recaptured within the past three days, most of whom were caught with hounds. Lieut. Parker was so torn by dogs that he died the next day after his capture.

On the 7th inst., Lieut. J. Clement, of the 15th Kentucky Cavalry, was captured by a rebel living but a short distance from Chapel's Ferry, South Carolina.

After the lieutenant had surrendered, the dogs were let loose on him, and thus he was so seriously injured as to be disabled for a long time.

I should have made my escape on the fourth, had not my health been in such a delicate state, that I could not have walked out of camp, even had the road been clear.

I have suffered much during the past two weeks with camp diseases, and am now so weak

Issuing Meat Rations at Camp Sorghum.

as to be unable to walk without the aid of a friend.

Nov. 12. It is rumored here that Gen. Sherman has left Atlanta, and is moving through Georgia in three columns. It is the current opinion that he will occupy Augusta. The Great General's movements are but little understood by the rebels; they are greatly alarmed and are concentrating their forces at Augusta. Quite an amusing scene enlivened the camp this afternoon. An old wild hog chanced to pass the guard line, and as soon as he came within range of the prisoners a general advance was made, and he was ours; but a few moments elapsed after the entrance of Mr. hog, before no traces of his carcass could be found; from four to five hundred half starved men were interested in the division of this small fry, hence it is not wonderful that our long-eared benefactor very suddenly disappeared.

My messmate, Richardson, was the first to seize a leg and did not quit his hold until it was cut off and securely lodged in a mess kettle for supper. This is the first and only ration of meat that we have had since our arrival at Columbia on the fifth of October.

"The black hog was seen running through camp:
Each man forgetting starvation and cramp,
Grunts of the hog and its running were vain —
Never he'll be on that camp ground again."
The Wandering Poet of New Hampshire.

Nov. 20. It is now very generally understood here that Sherman is moving through Georgia in three columns; he is supposed to be marching on Augusta, Macon, and Savannah. There were many attempts to escape during the fore part of last evening; several shots were fired into the pen by the sentinels; one of the prisoners had his arm blown off in an effort to run the guard. Weather cold, wet and disagreeable.

Nov. 23. Lieut. Geo. R. Barse, 5th Michigan Cavalry, of whom I have spoken in a previous note, made his escape this morning, while the prisoners were passing out on parole after wood.

The officer of the guard had taken position without the guard line where he had a battalion of men in readiness to send to the woods with the paroled prisoners, allowing several to go at a time, and proportioning the number of guards to the size of the squad.

As each party arrives near the "dead line," one of the number manifests a desire to pass out, at the same time exhibiting a paper with signatures attached to a written parole. The officer of the guard then beckons to the sentinel to permit them to cross the lines, when he takes their paroles and hands them to one of a certain number of armed men, who are detailed to act as their escort.

Barse followed a squad that observed all this necessary formality; but the officer and guard were none too bright; and Lieut. B. went on rejoicing no doubt at his good fortune until he reached the woods, when he claimed that he was a hospital steward, and had nothing to do with the men, whom he had only chanced to walk out of camp with. Luckily, there was no one present to contradict his assertion, and, without further ceremony, marched off at his pleasure.

GOV. BROWN'S PROCLAMATION.

We learned, through one of the sentinels, this afternoon that Gen. Beauregard and the Georgia legislature are at Macon. Gov. Brown has issued a proclamation, ordering to the front every man capable of bearing arms.

Thanksgiving Day, Nov. 24. There has been great suffering in camp during the past week, on account of the severity of the weather.

HEAVY FROSTS—NO BLANKETS.

We have heavy frosts very frequently. Many of the prisoners are still without blankets, and, to prevent chilling, are compelled to keep moving during the night. They sleep during the day, while warmed by the sun.

Messmates Hampton, Richardson and myself possess each a small blanket; but with even these, it is almost impossible to keep from freezing.

SLEEPING IN THE MIDDLE.

We sleep in the middle by turn; and this privilege with us is a matter of the gravest importance. So unpardonable is the offence of attempting to deprive one of his equal rights in this respect, that many quarrels have originated from no other source.

In a case involving so much interest, we do not trust to the memory, but, on turning out in the morning, mark upon the ground the name of the individual who is to have the choice of position at night. This method was not resorted to until we found it to be the only security against disputes.

The one who has the middle is usually quite comfortable; and hence we are sure of one night's rest in three, if not drowned out by a rain storm.

NO PROSPECT OF AN EXCHANGE.

Nov. 25. After awaiting our turn more than three weeks, we have at last succeeded in securing an old shovel, and are now digging a hole in the ground, which we shall crawl into at night and during storms.

There seems to be no prospect of a general exchange of prisoners, and we are determined to make the best of our miserable situation.

It is not the intention to spend a single night in this bear's den, if possible to effect an escape; but the prisoner has learned by experience, that it is always policy to be prepared for the worst.

RENEWED DETERMINATION TO ESCAPE.

As for myself, I shall say adieu to this "hell hole" to-morrow, if there is any such thing in the book.

I saw friend Lemon this morning, and proposed to him a plan for a leave taking of "Camp Sorghum."

As it is customary to extend the guard line in the morning, for the purpose of allowing the prisoners to pick up wood on a piece of timbered land just opposite camp, it is the intention to take a shovel when we are thus permitted to pass to the woods, and to make a hole in the ground large enough to receive two skeletons like our own, and then getting our friends to cover us with brush and leaves, we shall doubtless be left without the camp when the guard is withdrawn. Should we succeed in escaping the vigilance of the sentinels, we shall endeavor to reach Augusta, feeling assured that Gen. Sherman will soon occupy that place. Many have preferred to strike for Knoxville, Tennessee, considering that the safest, though it is much the longest route to our lines. We shall incur more risk, but if fortunate, will the sooner be within the Federal camp.

CHAPTER IX.

THE ESCAPE FROM COLUMBIA.*

First Day.

Lexington C. H. Road, six miles from Columbia,—*Nov.* 26, 1864.

Not having had access to the papers for some time past, in our pen at Columbia, we were, of course, in utter ignorance of the state of things without. Rumor, however — a daily which could not well be excluded — had informed us that Gen. Sherman was between Macon and Augusta; and believing him to be in need of recruits, I at once determined to offer him my services. Several prisoners being out on parole this morning, myself among the number, I observed one of the guard to be a stupid looking fellow, and proposed testing his abilities before he should

---

* Written during the escape, while in the swamps and cotton gins of South Carolina and Georgia, where we were secreted by the ever faithful negroes.

be relieved by one of brighter appearance. Accordingly, I hastened back to camp, had my parole revoked, and then hurried to the quarters of Lieut. M. W. Lemon, of the 14th N. Y. Heavy Artillery, a man of courage and enterprise, and one who would enter heartily into any plan for escape. I only told him to meet me at a certain point, and be ready to leave the pen in three minutes.

No time was lost in packing or checking our baggage to any given point; and we also deemed it unnecessary to bid our friends good bye, or to thank the proprietors for hospitalities received.

PASSING THE DEAD LINE.

We were soon at the specified place, passed up to the "dead line" as if that point possessed no further interest to us, and were in the act of stepping over, when the aforementioned worthy brought his gun to bear upon me with an uncomfortable precision; at the same time ordering a halt.

"Where are you going, Yanks?" he demanded; but, with an air of offended dignity, I only said, "Do you halt paroled prisoners here?" His meek "No, sir," was almost lost in the distance, as I boldly crossed the dreaded line, adding, "Then let the gentleman in the rear follow me;" and so we passed, while the brilliant sentinel murmured, "All right."

And right it was; for now we were free, breathing the fresh air, untainted by the breath of hundreds of famishing, diseased and dying men.

MEETING NEGROES.

The country, outside of cities and villages at the south, is always so sparsely settled that, once on the road, and no hounds upon the track, one can readily find places of concealment. Of course it was our policy at the first to keep comparatively scarce for a time; but soon after dark we struck the Lexington Court House road, and directly came upon a company of negroes, returning from work upon government fortifications.

They were three in number; and after assuring ourselves of their color, we agreed to make their acquaintance.

This was readily done after convincing them we were not rebels in disguise, although either one would have sworn he never saw a Yankee;

as it would have been death to him to have been found in our society.

One of the party, Ben Stedman by name, was soon secured as a guide; and, to avoid unpleasant surprises, we agreed upon keeping in his rear, as he would be always safe, while a recognition of ourselves would be neither safe nor pleasant.

BLIND ROADS.

We marched nearly twenty miles during the night, Ben assuring us that there were no pickets on the way. By some means we had left the highway and entered a blind road which came near giving us trouble. These blind roads are a regular institution at the south, for instead of leading to some town or village as at the north, one is suddenly brought up in some man's door yard, and is soon surrounded by all the members of the plantation.

We were about eighteen miles south of Columbia when

A PICKET OF EIGHT MEN,

but one of them awake, stopped our further progress. This one gave the challenge, "who comes there?" when our guide answered, "Friends," though Lieut. L. and myself were not coming in that direction at all, but flying in an opposite course as fast as our legs could carry us. Ben as we afterwards learned, made a good story about two other darkies being along, getting scared and running away, adding,

"I DUN NO WHAT MAKE DEM NIGGERS RUN SO."

His story being corroborated by those who had seen him leave the works, he was soon set at liberty, ready to do another good job when called for.

About an hour later we stumbled upon

ANOTHER PICKET

of five men, but being unable to flank them on account of a swamp, halted and slept near them until morning. We had eaten nothing save a small piece of corn bread since leaving Columbia, and had not dared to present ourselves before any habitation; but hoped to break our long fast after ten o'clock the next night.

Second Day.

Barnwell, C. H. Road, near Black Creek, S. C.,— *Nov.* 28.

We reached the junction of four roads at 12 o'clock last night, and fortunately found a friend in an old guide board. Jumping upon my companion's shoulders, I was enabled by the light of the moon to decide upon the course to be pursued.

We halted at two o'clock A. M. near the plantation of Alexander Taylor, and were made known of our proximity to that residence by the furious barking of a dog, about daylight.

I, for one, felt it unnecessary for him to apprise us that morning had arrived, and was at once upon my feet. Running I knew would be nonsense, especially as the planter's wife had been attracted by the tumult.

My companion preferred remaining at a safe distance from his dogship, while I approached the ladies who were already assembled near, and after learning there were no white men on the plantation, I frankly stated my case, and appealed to their sympathies for something to eat. They were at first unwilling to grant me

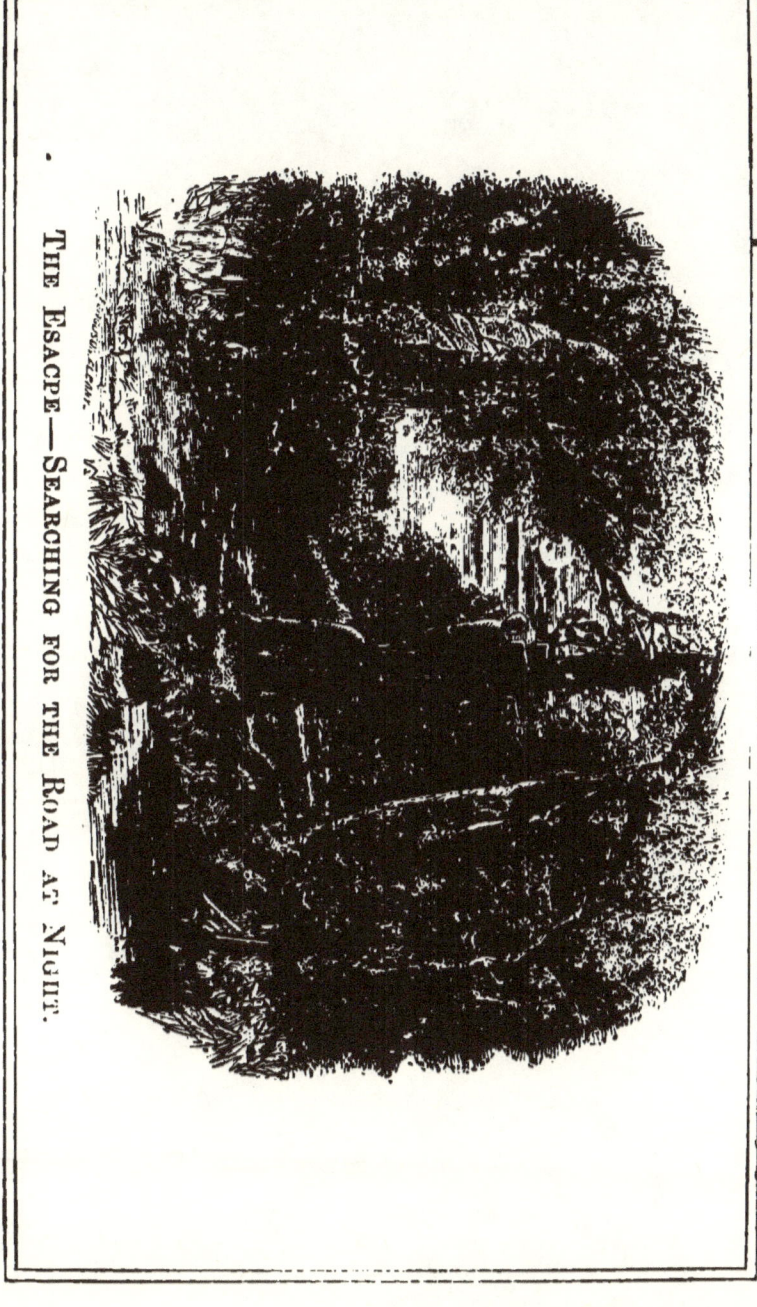

The Esacpe—Searching for the Road at Night.

any assistance. Mrs. Taylor said that her husband was in the Confederate army, that her heart was with the southern people, and further, that she thought it wrong for her to aid a Yankee in making his escape. I then addresssed to her a brief speech, recounting in pitiful terms my misfortunes, and my disappointment, should I fail in reaching Gen. Sherman's lines.

KINDNESS OF MRS. TAYLOR.

Mrs. Taylor made no reply to my soul-stirring speech other than "she would see what could be done for me;" which resulted in a generous supply of corn bread, bacon and sweet potatoes.

After extorting a promise from the ladies that they would not betray us, I promised Mrs. Taylor that if ever her husband came in Yankee hands, I would see that no harm befel him; and this promise I would have kept, even at the expense of my own life.

The rations were soon hurried into my haversack, and after again thanking my benefactress for her kindness, I returned to my companion, when we hastened off to a thicket in the woods, built a pine knot fire, roasted our potatoes and made

A ROYAL BREAKFAST.

Oh ye who sleep on beds of down in your curtained chambers, and rise at your leisure to feast upon the good things provided — smile not when I say you never knew the luxury of a night of rest, nor the sweets of a meal seasoned by hunger, and the grateful remembrance that it was provided by woman's kindly heart, which wherever it may beat, sooner or later responds to the tale of misfortune and suffering humanity.

A bath in a stream near by, with the washing of our stockings, completed the duties of the morning, and we were glad to rest, being weary, weak and sore, the result of violent walking.

I apprehend little danger of recapture, unless hounds are put on track, and as we travel only by night shall not be recognized; besides we proceed with the greatest caution.

Fourth Day.

Near North Edisto River, on the road to Aiken, S. C.,—*Nov.* 29.

We reached Black Creek this morning just before day break, and while crossing the bridge over said stream,

MET A NEGRO

on his way to work, who turned back and conducted us to a hut for safe keeping during the day.

This hut, familiarly known throughout the neighborhood as "Aunt Katy's," is the gathering place for all in want of assistance. In an incredibly short space of time all the blacks on the plantation were here assembled.

A PRAYER MEETING

was improvised for our especial benefit, and which was conducted in a manner both creditable to themselves and amusing to us. The burden of their petitions was, that all the prisoners held by the rebels might make a general exodus and reach the Yankee lines in safety; that we in particular might succeed in making our escape; and that our armies might speedily conquer the whole of Secessia, liberate the slaves, and take possession of the land.

As faith without works is of little avail, their next step was to make arrangements for our future.

It was now daylight, and we were advised to remain in our present quarters for the day, assuring us that "no white folks nebber come near Aunt Katy's. So, don't be afraid, Massa."

After the necessary instructions for our journey, which was to re-commence at ten o'clock P. M., they dispersed to their labors, promising to prepare our rations in time for us to proceed at that hour.

We left Black Creek at the appointed time with

A NEGRO GUIDE,

who, by the way, was a friend of Ben Stedman. Ben, he said, was taken prisoner, as before related; and, upon examination, told the plausible story aforementioned, that Lemon and myself were two foolish darkies who were scared at the pickets. The latter part of his narrative being strictly true, it was hardly necessary for us to rectify the former.

Ben was afterward brought to our hiding place in the thicket by his colored friend from Black Creek, and kindly offered his services for the occasion.

We told him we were anxious to learn of Gen. Sherman's movements, and would like a paper. He insisted upon our going to his hut, although we much preferred the swamp; but were at last prevailed upon to accompany him. Arriving here, we were politely introduced to Mrs. Stedman and family. They viewed a live Yankee with not a little curiosity; after which, Ben instructed his daughter to go into her mistres's house and snatch a paper at the earliest opportunity. She soon came running back with

THE "AUGUSTA CONSTITUTIONALIST,"

published this morning. The celerity with which the blacks carry off a desired article, or accomplish a mission for a friend, is truly wonderful; and no watchfulness on the part of their masters can stay a project when once the heart is in it.

CROSSING THE NORTH EDISTO.

Having possessed ourselves of the contents of the paper, we struck the road and crossed the North Edisto at ten o'clock P. M.

The water was over the bridge in many places. So we were compelled to ford the stream.

We intended to reach and cross the South Edisto before morning, but have become confused by the intersection of blind roads, and have concluded to halt.

Fifth Day.

On the South Edisto, Wednesday,—*November 30.*

Had a breakfast of hoe cake and pindars; the latter being known at the north as pea-nuts. Lieut. L. and myself were in great tribulation at day-break owing to the loss of our moorings. The blind road which we followed last night seemed to terminate in a swamp. There were no stars visible, and we had not yet learned to take the moon for a guide. Besides, the heavenly bodies at this season of the year, and in this latitude, have so different an appearance from those seen north that they confuse us. We are, therefore, "down the banks," and deem it policy to go no farther before ascertaining our whereabouts.

Here we remained until about ten o'clock, but saw no one, and concluded it was high time to change our base of operations, and find our colored friends again. So, taking a southeasterly direction, making the sun our guide, we proceeded, and many were the adventures and hair breadth escapes with which we met.

We struck the Aiken road at ten o'clock this evening, and have just crossed the South Edisto.

OTHER DIFFICULTIES.

We are not yet out of the swamp along the river, and shall be compelled to "lie low" until morning, as we have discovered pickets, and cannot flank them, as they have planted themselves in the road, and there is a pond on either side. Oh for some Moses to cut us a path through the deep, or a Sampson to disperse our foes until we can reach the promised land.

Sixth Day.

Aiken Road, seven miles south of the South Edisto,—*Dec.* 1.

Day-break found us in a bad situation. Pickets and plantation before us, and no water to be obtained.

An elevated table land, entirely destitute of water, was passed over, and, after walking seven miles, a good drink was the reward, and we were glad to rest awhile after quenching our thirst.

Here we lay concealed in a thicket until ten o'clock P. M., and then proceeded on our journey.

Seventh Day.

Four miles north of Aiken, }
Friday,— *Dec.* 2. }

We halted at day-light, about a mile from our present hiding place, near a stream of water, but were not destined to a long stay in so delightful a location; for, as Lemon was returning from the creek he espied a colored boy in the road, bearing a basket on his arm. "Hold on, my boy, I want to see you," he sang out; thinking, mean time, that the basket doubtless contained what we most needed, something of an eatable character.

We inferred the boy had a chicken with him; for saying that word, in a manner which betokened the greatest fear, he set off at a wild run, and I would have defied a race horse to catch him. As for the lieutenant, after exhausting all his rhetoric in endeavoring to bring back the boy, he returned to the spot where I lay, saying "Now they will have us again, and we shall be prisoners before night."

"Never fear," I said, "as long as there is a swamp in the neighborhood;" and, without further ceremony, we picked up our baggage and hastily decamped. Flora Temple would have been distanced had she attempted to overtake us; for her stakes would have been only a few dollars to her owners, while ours were life and liberty.

PURSUED BY BUSHWHACKERS.

Our present position gives us a good view of the road, while we cannot be seen by those passing below. Several old bushwhackers have gone down to Aiken, thinking no doubt, that the foolish Yankees of whom the colored boy has told them, will be so verdant as to pass through town to-night. But they will learn their mistake, as our intention is to flank them.

Eighth Day.

In a corn-fodder house, near Aiken, S. C.,— *Dec.* 3.

In spite of our intentions to the contrary, we were surprised to find ourselves in the village last evening. Soon after dark we struck the road, and found we had been but a short distance out when we thought ourselves four miles off. We passed hurriedly through on the main road to Augusta.

MEETING ESCAPED PRISONERS.

Here we met Capt. Bryant, of the 5th N. Y. Cavalry, and his companion. They were greatly alarmed at our approach and set off on a run, until we cried out, "Don't be uneasy Yanks, we are friends." I at once knew them to be escaped prisoners, and they seeing the same in us, returned, and briefly told us their adventures. They had a negro guide, who was to secrete them in a hut until night again, when they were to proceed as we had done, and reach the lines of freedom by the nearest route.

APPROACHING A NEGRO.

At daylight, L. and myself found ourselves in a swamp about a mile out of town.

The familiar sound of an ax now fell upon our ears, and cautiously approaching, I saw a colored boy cutting wood. I soon made myself known to him, told him my story, and asked for food and a place of secretion. He assured me he would do all in his power for Yankees, and after piloting us up to this fodder house, he went to the negro quarters and brought over a hoe cake and some bacon.

After dark a large number of colored boys and girls came up to pay their respects. They entertained us with their views of the war, and proposed a prayer meeting for our especial benefit; also told us where to look out for trouble from bushwhackers, hounds, and so forth. Our parting from these friendly people was tender and affecting; each one shaking hands, and saying "God bless you, massa."

Ninth Day.

Between Grantsville and Hamburg,
Sunday,—*December* 4.

We left Aiken at ten o'clock last night, and passed through Grantsville just as a freight train was leaving for Augusta. Tried hard to get a passage upon one of the cars, but found the doors all closed and locked. Our intention was to ride into Augusta, and, while it was still dark, make our way out of the city.

We had designed crossing the river below the city; but the blacks informed us that all the small boats were destroyed along the Savannah, to prevent the slaves escaping. This is a greater misfortune to us than them, as sooner or later they will be free; while with us, it is a matter of debate for some time to come.

We hope to take the cars at Hamburg before day-break to-morrow morning. This will be a dangerous undertaking, but I see no other way of getting into Georgia. It will not be necessary to procure tickets, or to have any acquaintance with the conductor; so we shall make that worthy as little trouble as possible.

GOOD MUSIC—GREATLY ENCOURAGED.

Heavy cannonading has been sounding in our ears all day. It comes from a southeasterly direction, and is the sweetest music we have heard for many an hour. It seems as if we were in the neighborhood of friends, and we take heart, feeling encouraged for the future.

FOLLOWED BY A HOUND.

A hound followed us for a mile or more this morning after we left Grantsville; but I think he barked upon his own responsibility, as he soon ceased, and gave up the chase.

Tenth Day.

Near Aiken and Charleston Railroad,
Monday,—*December* 5.

We have laid in a thicket since morning, and were greatly surprised to learn this evening that instead of taking the road for Augusta we were en route for Charleston—traveling east rather than south; and having not the least desire to visit the last named city. Our distance east of Aiken is seventeen miles; a bad mistake to be sure. But Providence seems still to favor us, as we learn, through our colored friends, that we can cross the Savannah twenty miles below Augusta, at a place called Point Comfort. Our army is now marching on Savannah. So we have rather gained than lost by our mistake.

This evening we are making for Tinker Creek; and, having been refreshed throughout the inner man, are in excellent spirits. We have secured a good stock of hoe cake and sweet potatoes, and have been posted in regard to the country as far as the river.

Eleventh Day.

Near Tinker Creek, S. C., Tuesday,—*December* 6.

The weather is very cold, and we suffer much from its severity. During the night we came to a fork in the road but a few rods from a plantation.

A RACE.

After debating for some time as to which road we should take, I jumped over the fence, and made for a negro hut, while several hounds from the plantation followed hard on my track. I managed, by some tall running, to come out ahead and get into the hut, at the same time bidding Cuffee to call in the dogs and make them lie down, which he accordingly did. While my colored friend was thus engaged, I had an opportunity of surveying the interior of his domicil.

SOMETHING FOR THE HAVERSACK.

What was most pleasing to my eyes, as well as olfactories, was a skillet of fresh pork, cooking over the fire, and a hoe cake in the ashes.

Without waiting for ceremony, or inquiring where my poor host would obtain another breakfast, I emptied the skillet into my haversack and snatched the half baked hoe cake from its warm resting place.

Cuffee of course understood my wants, and I only said, "Uncle, which road must this rebel take for Tinker Creek?" Again bidding him to have a care for the hounds until morning, I rushed out to the road and soon joined my companion.

Twelfth Day.

Near Point Comfort, Wednesday,—*December* 7.

We left Tinker Creek last evening at eight o'clock, and traveled fifteen miles with a guide. Halted at length near a large plantation, where we were advised to make the acquaintance of some colored boys, and engage them to take us down to the river. The blacks are everywhere our friends, and render us all the assistance in their power. To-day, while we were stowed away in a deep pit, a party of lads came within fifteen feet of our hiding place. They were out squirrel hunting, and came near finding larger game.

Made a breakfast of hoe cake and pindars, and supped on pindars without the hoe cake. Shall endeavor to cross the river to-night. Every day puts us further from our hated prison, and nearer Gen. Sherman's lines.

Thirteenth Day.

In a cypress swamp, on the Savannah, }
Thursday,— *Dec.* 8. }

We reached the Savannah at ten o'clock last night, and were so fortunate as to find a kind-hearted colored fisherman who was acquainted with every bend in the river; he had followed the river before the war, and now proposed taking up his old trade in our favor.

He carried cotton and pitch to a small tributary of the Savannah, where lay an old cypress tree canoe, which he had formerly used for fishing. It had recently passed under the boat-destroyer's notice, and had been pretty roughly handled.

VIEWING OUR LITTLE CRAFT BY MOONLIGHT.

When we first surveyed it by moonlight, I confess to a want of faith in its being able to carry us to the other side. Our faithful pilot worked ha d all night caulking and pitching her seams, until near daybreak, when he threw it into the stream, exclaiming, "Now she is ready massa, I will soon land you in Georgia."

BAILING FOR LIFE.

We hastily took our seats in the boat which was leaking fearfully, and while our pilot pulled for the opposite shore, L. and myself bailed for dear life, expecting every moment to go to the bottom. We reached the opposite shore just as our old craft was full, jumped into near two feet of water and pulled the boat after us.

When we started for the swamp, our good friend was patiently wadding his old canoe with cotton, preparatory to a return to his home. May he get there in safety, and carry many another poor fellow on his way rejoicing. It is late in the afternoon, and we have become bewildered in the swamp, and apprehend difficulty in reaching the highlands. We are surrounded by an innumerable number of streams and pond holes, while a number of

ALLIGATORS

have been watching our motions, apparently pleased at our misfortunes, and sending loving glances in this direction. They too may belong to some detachment of Southern Chivalry, and are doing duty on their own grounds.

Fourteenth Day.

Near Brier Creek, Georgia, }
Friday,— *December 9.* }

Found our way out of the swamp last night, by taking

THE NORTH STAR

as our guide. How many a wanderer has found his home, and how many a prisoner his release, by following this never erring guide. No wonder the heathen nations bow down in admiration and worship before the heavenly bodies, and many a weary pilgrim, in more enlightened lands, feels like rearing an altar to the pole star of his freedom. We traveled fourteen miles last night, and to-day are again concealed in a swamp, where we can see all that passes, though no one can see us, unless some enquiring hound should scent our whereabouts, and publish the news to his master. I have a notion that even the dumb animals in this Godless country have a peculiar instinct of what is required of them, and are rewarded accordingly.

We have as yet no information of Gen. Sherman's army. The bridges across all the principal streams are destroyed, or heavily guarded. A large

CAVALRY PATROL

passed near us to-day, so we keep quiet and eat our sweet potatoes raw, they being the only rations we have, and a fire out of the question. How good a breakfast at home would taste just now, and how willingly the dear ones there would furnish it. It would be no common meal, each one would strive to bring the sweetest morsel, and I should ache with a surfeit, where I now feel a vacant, unsatisfied longing.

Found an old darkey splitting rails near our hiding place this morning. He has agreed to bring us some hoe cake, and best of all, thinks he can repair

MY OLD SHOES.

These shoes, like many other unimportant looking things, have a history. Shortly after my capture I was relieved of my cavalry boots, and a pair of pasted shoes given me, which yielded to the first moisture and left me worse than barefoot. A fellow prisoner having received a remittance of good things from home, among them a pair of boots, kindly presented me with his shoes. Smile not gentle reader at the gift, for to me they were invaluable; and with these I marched many weary miles, although they were patched and wired together until little remained of their former substance, and now they were well nigh gone. Cuffee took them home, and spent the greater part of the night in making them answer their appointed end. A piece of possum skin formed the uppers, and were nicely tucked under. A slit at the instep admitted the foot; but I was forced to find fault with my colored cobbler for this breach, though I soon learned, not from him alone, but from experience, that the darkey knew best, for the skin of the possum, though soft and pliable when moist, is soon harder than sheet iron or any other of its kindred metals. My feet are sore, and suffer much from their nightly ablutions in two or three feet of swamp water.

Fifteenth Day.

Near Godbey's Bridge, five miles from Alexander, Ga., Saturday,—*December* 10.

The weather is rainy, and we are suffering much from cold and exposure. Could not move last night on account of the rain, and still pursue our swamp life.

Have had nothing to eat to-day, save an ear of dry corn, picked up on an old camping ground, and refused by some aristocratic horse. A detachment of Wheeler's Cavalry passed here yesterday morning. We shall move toward Millin to-night.

Sixteenth Day.

Between Station No. 1 and Millin, Ga., Sunday,—*December* 11.

Weather cold and rainy still, and we are obliged to run to make ourselves comfortable.

We left Godbey's Bridge last night at eight o'clock, and traveled until day-light. Made about twenty miles, and are very hungry and weary this morning. The roads are in a bad condition. Mud deep, and the streams much swollen.

FORDING STREAMS AND BACKING EACH OTHER.

We took off our shoes and forded four large creeks. L. and myself agreed upon carrying each other over these bridgeless torrents; and I selfishly took the first rides, hoping each one would be the last. My turn, however, at length arrived. So, shouldering the mighty lieutenant, as boys at school pay their forfeits, I plunged into the water, and resolutely bore my burden to the deepest point, when, through no fault of mine, the depth was either too great, or I, poor boy, too short to keep the worthy gentleman's feet dry; and the consequence was, he got a thorough soaking, and afterward chose to do his own wading, though often lending me a helping hand through the worst places. The lieutenant could swim, but I could not.

Seventeenth Day.

In a swamp on the Savannah River Road, Monday,—*December* 12.

We did not commence our tramp until near day-light to-day. The weather is so cold, and the water so high, that little can be gained by moving.

We are, evidently, on Gen. Sherman's line of march, though he is six days in advance of us. Would the good man halt awhile if he knew we were in pursuit of him? I think, from his kind heart, he would at least send out a small detachment for us; and then how gladly we would ride into camp, and how willingly share the fortunes of his brave legions in their triumphant march to the sea. We have been in motion nearly all day; and, besides, have been chased by hounds. If the wretches knew how little there is left of us, I think they would give up the pursuit as fruitless. Next to a good meal for ourselves, a small amount of strychnine and fresh meat would be our most desirable offering to the dogs; and I would advise all future travelers to go prepared with that commodity.

Eighteenth Day.

Sixty miles north of Savannah, Tuesday.—*December* 13.

We started out last evening at eight o'clock, and are still following the line of our own army. We are without food, and sorely pressed with hunger. Now and then we find an ear of corn, left by the rebel cavalrymen. Last evening we stopped at a plantation, and, seeing no plantation house, concluded they were all negro huts. Approaching the most respectable looking one, I rapped at the door, when some one sang out, "Whose thar?" From the answer, I was unable to guess whether the occupants were black or white, and accordingly said, "Are you black or white in there?" The answer: "There aint no niggers here;" and the very indignant tone satisfied me that I had fallen upon some "poor white trash," as they are here familiarly called.

ACTING THE PART OF A REBEL.

Determined to have something to eat, at all events, besides being anxious to learn something of our course, I assumed a tone of offended dignity and summoned the speaker to the door. I demanded, in the name of an injured rebel officer, why he was not forthcoming at once.

Upon meeting "mine host," I soon found he had seen his best days; and feeling quite at home, asked how long since our army had passed.

"What army," he enquired, as if to make sure of no mistake. "The rebel army of course," I replied. He then told me Wheeler's Cavalry had passed a week since, in pursuit of Sherman's rear guard.

Can you tell me how far it is to Wheeler's Head Quarters?" I asked. "Indeed I cannot," he answered, "but I reckon its a right smart distance sir."

"Are there any horses or mules in the neighborhood?" I asked. "Not one," he replied, "the cursed Yankees have cleaned us out, and done gone with our last piece of bread."

"Well, come now uncle' can't you give this rebel something to eat?" "No," he returned, "there is not a mouthful in the pantry, we are whipped clean out."

"I know better sir," I said — "you have bacon and sweet potatoes, you must shell out or I shall have to help myself." Rebel wishing to shirk the responsibility of a falsehood from his own shoulders, called to Mrs. Rebel to know if there was anything eatable on the premises; to which she replied, "I reckon you will find something in the pantry;" and in a moment more my rebellious friend returned with a small bit of bread and two sweet potatoes.

After receiving which, I delivered him a lecture upon his treatment of a soldier who had ventured all upon the defense of his country; telling him he was unworthy the cause he had espoused, and that his patriotism did not reach to his pockets, to say nothing of his falsehood and mean attempts to defraud me of a breakfast. "Hoping, I added, to find you a better rebel when we meet again,"—I hurried off to L., who was still waiting by the road, and shared our hard earned meal with an appetite well whetted by hunger.

Pushing on at a rapid pace in the direction of our army, we spied a person crossing the road a short distance before us, and as the whites seldom stir before daylight, our first conclusion was that we had found a colored friend, but were soon undeceived by discovering a burly looking white man. After passing the compliments of the morning, we inquired how long since our cavalry passed. "Last Tuesday," he replied; and not wishing to detain him, we proceeded on our way, grateful that our uniforms were hidden under our blankets, which answered at once as overcoats and a good disguise.

Leaving planter No. 2, to his own reflections,

we reached a swamp at daybreak. Here met two negroes going to their work, and after a "Good morning boys," inquired the distance to the next plantation.

"Just a mile from this swamp, massa."

"Are there any white people there?" we asked.

"Not one massa,

DE PLANTER WAS A BUSHWHACKER

and Mr. Sherman's company took em all off."

Wishing to have my stories of the morning agree, and not knowing how soon they would be tested, I did not think it necessary to make myself known to my colored friends, but asked whether they had seen any of Wheeler's Cavalry of late.

"There's a right smart of 'em down at Massa Brown's, three miles from the swamp, and dey's hazin about de country in ebery direction." Feeling a little uneasy after the above information, we started for the plantation described. As we hove in sight, I saw the house was closed, but that smoke was rising from a hut in the grounds—so made for it in double quick time; walked up to, and opened the door without hesitation, when, to my surprise and horror, I beheld

A CONFEDERATE OFFICER,

standing before the fire. Without the least hesitancy I advanced, gave him the military salute and said, I see you, too, are in the service, sir; but hope, like myself, you have not been unfortunate.

MY HORSE, SHOT AT WAYNESBORO.

"How unfortunate may you have been, sir?" he asked. Now I might have stated all the mishaps of my life; but only quietly said, "I was in the cavalry fight at Waynesboro the other day, had my horse shot from under me, failed to get re-mounted, and have walked the entire distance to this place."

"I reckon our cases are not unlike, after all," he rejoined; "I had my horse shot there, too, but luckily got a mule;" and, stepping to the door, he pointed out his long-eared animal, eating hay at the gate.

TRANSFERRED.

Fearing he might get the start of me, I asked to what command he belonged.

"The 53d Alabama Mounted Infantry," he returned; and then inquired my regiment.

"The 3d South Carolina Cavalry," I said; and true it was, that my last service was in that state. I occupied his time a few moments in recounting the barbarities of Gen. Sherman's army, remarking, "Now we have him just where we want him—between two swamps; and when he is thoroughly starved out we shall catch him easy enough."

OUR CLOTHING EXCITES SUSPICION.

The lieutenant seemed to endorse my remarks, notwithstanding my blue clothes; and just as I thought his suspicions fully allayed he remarked, "that it was strange for a gentleman of my professions to be dressed in Federal colors."

I returned, "It is not strange at all, sir." A poor fellow must wear what he can get in these times. I have not had a full equipment since I came into the service, and never expect one." You know, in the fight at Waynesboro we captured a few Yanks; and I just stripped a dead one, and appropriated his attire to myself.

"A good idea," he said, pointing to his tattered pants; "wish I had been as sensible."

DETERMINED TO HAVE A BREAKFAST.

My poor stomach had gained nothing during this interview, so I asked, "Do you suppose Aunty could give me some breakfast?"

"I reckon not, stranger," he returned; the Yanks have done gone with all the corn on this plantation; but if you will go down to

MR. BROWN'S,

you can get all you ask for. He was a good Union man when Gen. Sherman passed through, and on that account had a guard set over his property; then, when our army came along he was all Secesh."

"Well, sir, I shall be at Mr. Brown's without delay, and shall be happy to breakfast with you there. How far do you call it over there?"

"About two sights and a jambye," he returned, in true rebel parlance.

The good officer also informed me it was fifty-two miles to Savannah, twenty-five to Wheeler's Head Quarters, and about thirty-five to the rear of Sherman's army; adding, "Its a smart walk you'll have I reckon."

With a hearty "Thank you sir, and a good morning, we shall meet you at Mr. Brown's," we left him, and kept the road until entirely out of his range, when we suddenly struck into a swamp.* Messrs. Brown & Co. may be still waiting that breakfast for us, for ought I know; may they wait and watch with due patience.

Eighteenth Day.

In a Swamp near the Savannah,
Wednesday,—*Dec.* 14.

We were compelled to leave our place of concealment yesterday before dark, as L. was accidentally seen by a planter in search of a runaway negro. The planter gruffly asked, "What are you doing here in a blue uniform?" The lieutenant replied, "I am serving my country, as every loyal man should be."

Planter replied, "I believe you are a damned Yankee."

Lieut. L. returned the gallant answer of "Then you may think so;" but this interview placed us in

---

* Here we met negroes who had deserted their masters, and who kindly shared their rations with us.

A CRITICAL SITUATION,

and we suddenly decamped, while Mr. Planter started out to alarm the neighborhood. Taking the sun for a guide we set off in a southeasterly direction, and did not venture a halt before dark. We were

PURSUED BY HOUNDS

for more than two miles, but struck a stream of water, and waded up a half mile to evade our pertinacious followers.

This morning we found a small piece of pork in Sherman's camp, also a few ears of corn; all we have had for two days past. It has been impossible to find anything to eat since coming in line of the army. To use a southern phrase, the country is cleaned out; what the Federals left, the rebels have taken.

Nineteenth Day.

In a Swamp, near Big Ebenezer Creek,
Thursday,— *December* 15.

The creek was crossed under rather peculiar circumstances. After our misfortune yesterday of being recognized by a citizen, we made twenty miles, passing several pickets and patrols in safety. Arriving at the creek, we found the bridge burned, and returned to the swamp to take observations.

DUPING REBEL COURIERS.

My companion soon reported the stealthy sound of oars, and we had the pleasure of seeing two couriers tie a boat a few rods down the shore. After they were fairly out of sight we quietly took seats in the boat and pulled for the other side. Here we discovered the body of a dead cavalryman. He was one of our own men, and rather than he should go unburied, we gently laid him in the water — sent our boat down stream, and soon found the horses left by the couriers tied to a tree. Appropriated the horses for a couple of miles, and quickly made for this swamp, where we can distinctly hear the conversation of a neighboring picket.

CHAPTER X.

RE-CAPTURED BY A REBEL PICKET.

Twenty-first Day.

Twenty-five miles from Savannah, Saturday,—*December* 16, 1864.

"What potent spirit guides the raptured eye,
To pierce the shades of dim futurity?
Can wisdom lend, with all her Heavenly power,
The pledge of joy's anticipated hour?
Ah, no! she darkly sees the fate of man —
Her dim horizon bounded to a span;
Or, if she hold an image to the view,
'Tis Nature, pictur'd too severely true."

But a few hours have passed since L. and myself were stealing cautiously towards that goal for which we had so long and patiently struggled in the dismal swamps of South Carolina and Georgia.

Our hearts beat high with delight, as we felt that we were nearing the Federal lines; for we well knew that at the utmost, it could be but a few hours' walk to Sherman.

We left our place of concealment near Big Ebenezer creek at ten o'clock last evening, under the most deplorable circumstances, having been without rations for more than thirty-six hours, and being unable to obtain either guides or information concerning the situation of the armies.

We were, in fact, groping about like blind men, driven from point to point by the yelping of hounds or the movements of troops.

We reached the Little Ebenezer at about eleven o'clock P. M., and found the bridge destroyed. After reconnoitering a few moments, to ascertain, if possible, whether there was a picket on the opposite bank, we became satisfied that the coast was clear, and, constructing a raft out of such boards as we could find, made our way across the stream.

We then proceeded very cautiously, examining closely all the old camping grounds for crumbs of hard bread, and any other rations which might have been left by our army; for we were now on the Savannah river road, over which Kilpatrick's Cavalry and the 14th Army Corps had passed but a week before.

CHALLENGED BY A PICKET.

It was just as we were about turning from the road for the above mentioned purpose, that we were challenged in a very gruff tone of voice,

"Who comes there?"

I had long ere this decided upon the course to be pursued in case that we should be so unfortunate as to run upon a picket; and being too near the challenger to make running a safe expedient, I answered without hesitation,

"Friends."

Upon which the picket commanded "Advance one."

I advanced promptly, and, arriving near my captors, found them to be mounted infantrymen. They were sitting upon their horses in the shade of some large cypress trees.

ACTING AS SCOUT TO GEN. HARDIE.

One asked, "Who are you?" To which I replied, "I am a scout to Gen. Hardie and must not be detained, as I have important information for the general.

Sentinel. I am instructed to take every person to the officer of the picket that approaches this post after dark.

"I can't help it sir, it is not customary to arrest scouts and I must pass on."

"You cannot, I must obey orders. I do not doubt the truth of your assertion, but until you have seen the lieutenant, you will not be allowed to pass this post."

Finding that I had met a good soldier, I saw that it was useless to trifle with him, and tried to console myself with the thought that I should be able to dupe the lieutenant, and as we were hurried on toward the reserve of the picket, my mind was occupied in arranging a plan for our defence as spies to the great "Rebel Chief."

Reaching the reserve, we found nearly all asleep, in close proximity to a large rail fire, including my antagonist the lieutenant, he being roughly shook by one of the men, soon became sensible of his unconscious state, and rubbing his eyes for a moment, asked.

"What is wanted?"

I answered, "I am surprised sir, that scouts to our generals should be arrested by your picket."

He said, "My instructions are positive, and no man can pass this post without examination."

"Very well then," said I, "Be good enough to examine us at once."

"Have you passes?"

"No sir, not at present, we had passes when we left the general's head quarters, but having been scouting about in Northern Georgia for the past two weeks, our passes are worn out and lost."

"You have some papers about you, I suppose?"

Thinking that by answering in the affirmative, and producing quickly an old package of letters which had been received while in Libby Prison, that none of them would be criticised, I hastily drew them from the side pocket of my jacket and held them before me, saying, "I hope here are enough sir."

The lieutenant's curiosity led him to take one which had been received from Col. C. Buel, of Troy.

REGARDED AS A YANKEE SPY.

He held it near the fire, and noticing the date, turned his eyes towards me and again to the letter; the second glance seemed to satisfy him that I was not a rebel, and he remarked very indignantly, "Then you are scouting for Gen. Hardie, are you? I believe you are a damned Yankee spy, and if you were to get your just deserts, I should hang you to the first tree I come to." Said I, "Lieutenant do not be too hasty, I can convince you that I have been a prisoner of war, and if you are a true soldier, I shall be treated as such."

The lieutenant becoming a little more mild, gave us to understand, that we would be started for Springfield at ten o'clock, the head quarters of Gen. Wheeler.

After detailing a special guard for the prisoners, and instructing them to be on the alert, the lieutenant laid himself down by the fire, leaving us to reflect upon the hardness of fate, and the uncertainties attending an effort to escape the clutches of a barbarous enemy.

I soon found an opportunity to speak to Lemon, and communicated to him my intention to make another attempt to reach the Federal lines. I told him that I did not know what he had determined to do, but as for myself, I should never return to South Carolina a prisoner. I recounted to him the horrors and frightful consequences of prison life, and the privations and long suffering attending our attempt to escape from the hands of our unmerciful enemies; I told him that in my estimation it was quite as well to be hung by "bushwhackers," or torn to pieces by hounds in Georgia, as to return to South Carolina to meet a miserable death from the effects of starvation and exposure.

The lieutenant seemed to agree with me in every particular, and although he made no decisive answer, I concluded that I could count upon his coöperation. While with the picket, we learned that we had been arrested at the outpost, and that if we had been so fortunate as to have passed this post, we might have reached Gen. Sherman's lines in less than an hour. This intelligence was very disheartening indeed, when we saw that but a step intervened between suffering and happiness. Still I endeavored to look upon the bright side of the picture, thinking that if I could but have another chance in the "swamps," that I should be more successful.

A KIND ACT.

I shall never forget the kindness of James Brooks, one of the pickets, who came to us a little after daybreak, and asked if we would like some hoe cake and bacon (he said that he had been out "prowling," and would share his rations with the prisoners); we answered in the affirmative as a matter of course, having been without food for more than forty-eight hours, save a few ears of corn which we had been so fortunate as to find by the roadside, where the cavalrymen had fed their horses. In a moment more the hoe cake was forthcoming, much to the disgust of our friend's comrades, who called him "Blue Belly," and said he must be a fool to give his bread to the damned "Yanks." He made no reply to their insults, but set before us a most excellent breakfast.

AN ATTEMPT TO BRIBE THE GUARD.

After we had finished the hoe cake and bacon, I asked permission to pass under guard, to a little stream of water which was in sight of, and but a few rods from the reserve.

The favor was granted, and after we had taken a bath, I endeavored to bribe the guard by offering them one hundred dollars in "Confederate scrip" (which had been given me by the negroes), if they would give us an opportunity to make our escape.

They said that they would be right glad to have the money, but feared the consequences, as they were held responsible for our return. I told them that if they would listen to me, I would show them how they could make a good pile of Confed., and have no fears of punishment.

As we could be easily seen by the picket, my plan was to apparently take advantage of the guard by setting off at a run for the swamps, when they were to turn in pursuit, and without taking aim, fire in our direction.

I was confident that the scheme would work admirably, but the guards seemed to distrust each other, and instead of acceding to my proposition, they marched us back to the picket, and reported that we had attempted to bribe them. The lieutenant ordered a search at once, and what little scrip had been given us by our colored friends was soon in the hands of the "grey jackets." We were also threatened with severe punishment; one said, "shoot the damned Yankees," another,

"LET 'EM STRETCH HEMP."

Several reckoned that they had better take us into the *swamp*, and send us after Sherman's raiders; referring, I suppose, to the manner in which they had disposed of some of our sick that had necessarily been left in rear of the army; for before our re-capture, we were told by the negroes that fifteen of our sick that fell into the hands of the rebels but a few days since were taken to a swamp, where their throats were cut, and their bodies thrown into a slough hole.

I cannot vouch for the truth of this statement; but it came to me from many whose veracity I had no reason to doubt.

Our guard was universally applauded for their fidelity; but I am thoroughly convinced that if either had been alone, he would have thanked me for the suggestion and pocketed the money.

We remained with the picket until ten o'clock A. M., when a guard, consisting of a corporal and two men, were detached from the 6th Kentucky Cavalry, for the purpose of taking us to Gen. Wheeler's head-quarters.

APPARENTLY UNABLE TO WALK.

We had not proceeded far, however, when very suddenly I became so foot sore as to render it seemingly impossible for me to walk, which I claimed was the result of my long tramp since my escape from Columbia.

ONCE MORE IN THE SADDLE.

I affected to be too weak to mount without assistance, and allowed "Jonny reb" to help me into the saddle. It was not long before we came to some little trees by the roadside, and, riding under one, I broke off a small limb which I thought might be of some service in the future; for I was no sooner in the saddle than I had decided to effect my escape by flight, and determined to watch my opportunity.

I had rode the rebel charger but a short distance when my guard espied a black squirrel a few rods from the road. Forgetting the responsibility of his detail, he set off at a wild pace after the squirrel, which, after darting off a short distance, ran up a tree, and then, as if to show his superiority over Blondin, leaped from limb to limb with an expertness creditable to his species. His follower was upon the point of giving up the chase as a poor investment, when, suddenly, the little fellow halted and perching himself upon a limb, seemingly bade defiance to pursuit. I could not help regarding this little animal with some favor; for it appeared that he was about to sacrifice his life to my interests.

THE ESCAPE AND PURSUIT.

The carbine was instantly brought to the shoulder, and its report told me that then was my time, while the piece was unloaded; and, without waiting to mark the result of the shot, I whipped up and dashed off at a fearful rate, urging my charger to the top of his speed.

I was noticed immediately by the corporal, who left the other guard with Lemon, and came after me in a manner that was not the most flattering to my prospects. He was armed with a Colt's revolver, and while in pursuit discharged its contents at my unfortunate self, ordering me to halt at every shot. I paid no attention to the summons, but continued to urge my pony to his utmost. His time, however, at the best was quite unsatisfactory to my wishes; for had he been more fleet, I could have distanced the corporal, dismounted, and got into the swamps unobserved; but in this respect I was unfortunate, and was soon surprised to find myself approaching a camp, which was situated on both sides of the road. I turned my horse, leaped a fence, and endeavored to make my way across an open field; but the corporal's demand to halt the damned Yankee, was responded to by not less than fifty Texan rangers from the rebel Gen. Iverson's Cavalry Division. They came hooting and yelping, mounted and dismounted, armed and unarmed. Several blazed away at me with carbines and revolvers, but without effect.

I was, however, soon overtaken by fresh horses, and compelled to surrender myself once more a prisoner of war into the hands of the Texans.

The guard whom I thought so kind, and whose horse I had thus unmercifully ridden, came up in time to heap a most fearful tirade of curses upon me before we again resumed march. L. joined me a short time after my adventure, and we were then forced to walk the entire distance—our new guard having no sympathy for my lameness or debilitated condition.

ARRIVAL AT WHEELER'S HEAD-QUARTERS.

We reached Gen. Wheeler's head-quarters late in the afternoon, and the corporal reported to the general that he was in charge of two prisoners that had attempted to pass the outpost as scouts to Gen. Hardie. Wheeler ordered us into his presence, questioned us closely, and ordered our clothing searched. This investigation over, we were sent to our present quarters—a 10 by 15 cell in the county jail—where we are informed that we are to await a trial as Yankee spies. It would seem to be an easy matter to prove our identity as escaped prisoners of war; but the fact that I wore a grey jacket at the time of my re-capture, and that we represented ourselves as scouts to a Confederate general, make our captors very suspicious. I shall ever remember our interview with Gen. Wheeler; for it was quite an amusing scene, and illustrates, to some extent, the character of that rebel cavalry chief, whose career in the south and west has made his name so famous in the history of the rebellion. He first said to us,

"Then you are scouting for Confederate generals, are you?"

I replied, "We would have rejoiced could we but have convinced your outpost that we were—

W. Enough of your impudence, sir. Remember that you are a prisoner.

G. Very true; but when you ask questions you may anticipate answers.

W. What are you doing with that grey jacket?

G. I wear it, sir, to protect myself from the sun and storm.

W. Where did you get it?

G. One of the guard at Columbia was kind enough to give it to me, when he saw that I was suffering for the want of clothing with which to cover my shivering frame.

W. He could not have been a true rebel, thus to assist a Yankee in making his escape.

G. He knew nothing of my intention to escape; and I believe he was, at least, a sympathizing, kind hearted man.

W. Why don't you wear the Federal uniform? Is it possible that the Yankees are ashamed of the blue?

G. By no means, sir. What few garments were spared me at the time of my capture were worn out during a long imprisonment, and the clothing which was sent on to Richmond by our government during the winter of '63 for distribution among the prisoners was, for the most part, appropriated by your authorities.

W. Like many others of the contemptible Yankee crew, I believe you to be a lying scoundrel, and you shall answer to the charge of spy.

G. Very well sir, I am compelled to await your pleasure, but you have heard nothing but the truth.

W. Guard, take the prisoners to the jail, place them in a cell, and keep them in close confinement until further orders.

Twenty-first Day.

County Jail, Springfield, Ga.,
Saturday,—*December* 17.

Springfield is a very pleasant little village on the Middle Ground road. It is the county seat of Effingham county, and before the war contained several fine public buildings, which have recently been laid in ruins by the hostile armies.

We are at present the only military prisoners confined in the jail, which is temporarily in the hands of the military. The authorities were kind enough to allow us to leave our cell this morning and go out into the open air in front of the jail. The news spread rapidly that there were

"TWO LIVE YANKS IN THE JAIL YARD."

The citizens became alarmed and enraged to think that we should be permitted to leave the cell, and threatened to take the keys into their own hands, if we were not taken back.

The officer in charge told them that he was personally responsible for our safe keeping, and that they need not give themselves any uneasiness.

A large crowd gathered around and looked upon us with seeming wonder. Seeing that we appeared quite harmless, several ventured up to us and asked many curious questions. I found them to be the most ignorant class of people that I have ever met in the south. Many of them have supposed, until very recently, that the Yankees actually wore horns.

Their ideas of the war were laughable in the extreme.

Twenty-second Day.

Middle Ground Road, Twenty miles north of Springfield, Sunday,—*Dec.* 18.

Our farce of a trial being over at Springfield, in which we clearly proved our identity as prisoners of war. A heavy guard was detailed from the 2d Ga. Cavalry, with instructions to proceed with us to Waynesboro, together with fifteen prisoners from our 14th Army Corps, who were captured while out on a foraging expedition a few days since.

From them I have gained much valuable information concerning the situation of our army.

I have also learned where the rebel troops are stationed in Gen. Sherman's rear. Such information will be very important to me if I can but make my escape again..

As yet no rations have been issued to us since our recapture.

The rebel troops depend entirely upon foragers for their supplies, and seem to care but little for the wants of prisoners. A few ears of corn is all that we have had to keep soul and body together for several days.

I am in very low spirits to-night, which is owing to the fact that I have been foiled in every attempt to escape the vigilance of the guard during the day. I first urged the prisoners to straggle, so as to lengthen the column as much as possible, thinking that if we were permitted so to do, that I might succeed in dodging into a swamp unobserved; but the vigilant sergeant was too shrewd to be duped in this manner, and instructed his men to keep us closed up.

Failing in this scheme, I hoped that the sergeant would continue to march us during the night, in which case I could take advantage of the darkness and make off at my pleasure; but in this plan also I was destined to be disappointed; for much against my wishes we came to a halt but a few moments after dark, and were hurried into the old building which we now occupy.

Just before halting we had passed through a large swamp, where the water was so deep in the road as to compel each man to use his own discretion in making his way through.

The guard did its best to keep us together and prevent escapes; but in spite of their exertions one of our enlisted men fell out, whose absence was soon noticed by the sergeant.

METHOD OF ACCOUNTING FOR ABSENTEES.

We succeeded in convincing him that all the prisoners were present with whom he had started from Springfield. Our programme was thus: I found out the absent man's name; and then, as the sergeant had a list of the prisoners, I volunteered to call the roll for him. Getting us into a safe position, and lighting a piece of fat pine, he handed me the list, and I proceeded to call the names; as a matter of course, all who were present answered promptly, and then (according to previous instruction) as no one had heard such a name as the absent man bore, the sergeant concluded that it must have found its way upon the roll through mistake.

Under ordinary circumstances, I should be far from volunteering to aid a rebel in verifying his details; but in this case, I thought that by a little ingenuity, a fellow sufferer might return to liberty; for had not this scheme been devised, strenuous efforts would have been made by the guard to insure his capture. Picked men would have been detailed, hounds called out, and a few hours, at the furthest, would doubtless have convinced the unfortunate victim how little hope there is for him who seeks to shun the horrors of prison life by an escape.

We have all been entertained this evening by the good humor of one of the guard, who, having seen something of the world, is inclined to make light of the verdant, and somewhat peculiar speeches of his more unfortunate fellow Georgians, who have never passed the limits of the dismal swamps that surround their dreary homesteads. A story was told by this jovial cavalier, which he claimed was given him by an old lady to whom he had applied for bread during the day. It is designed to show her appreciation of Gen. Wheeler. She struck out as follows:

"Mr. Wheeler and his critter company drove into my back yard tother day, tipped my ash-hopper over, and formed a streak of fight half a mile long, and when he went away took off all my fowls, and never offered to pay me a dime. I had always thought before that yeuns (you) was a better set of men; but I begin to think that you are about as bad as the Yanks, after all."

Twenty-third Day.

Near Sylvania, Georgia,
Tuesday,—*Dec.* 19.

Commenced march at day-break this morning; since which time we have made twenty-five miles.

Sylvania is a small town, and, to all appearances, of but little importance. It is situated on the Middle Ground road, midway between Springfield and Waynesboro. The armies did not halt here; and, consequently, the people know but little of the sad realities resulting from the devastating tread of armed hosts. They are generally disposed to be talkative and friendly. Many of them are now conversing with the guard and prisoners. This suits me; for the guard cannot be vigilant when occupied in entertaining civilians. We are at present stationed on the porch of a large unoccupied building and the guard is posted in our front in the form of a semi-circle.

GOOD NEWS.

Soon after halting the sergeant came to me and said, my foragers have found some corn bread and sweet potatoes, which you see at the other end of the porch. I will give you all some potatoes and keep the bread for the guard.

Said I, silently, if we are permitted to remain without the building till dark, your guard will get but little of the bread, unless it is issued soon.

A FAVOR.

I then asked the sergeant if he would not be kind enough to allow us to remain outside until after supper (as it would be convenient for us to bake our potatoes in the rail fire which had just been built). The desired favor was granted, and I entered at once upon my plan for escape

CHAPTER XI.

THE ESCAPE FROM SYLVANIA, GEORGIA.

Twenty-fourth Day.

Wednesday,—*December* 20, 1864.

Having been told by the sergeant that we would be allowed to remain without the building until after supper, I called the attention of Lieut. J. W. Wright, 10th Iowa Vols.,* who was conversing with a citizen, and asked him if he had not better get his potatoes. I at the same time gave him a look, which he understood to mean a change of base. Hastily withdrawing from the citizen he met me on the porch, where I communicated to him my plan for escape, and enquired if he would join me in its execution. He replied without hesitation that he was up to anything but going back to South Caro-

---

* Circumstances prevented the escape of Lemon, my former companion, and he was taken back to Columbia.

lina, and would not shrink from bearing a hand in any move which I might make.

I will here say that Lieut. Wright was also an escaped prisoner from Columbia, whom I had often met during my imprisonment; he left Columbia a few days after Lieut. Lemon and myself, but unfortunately, like us, was recaptured at a time when he felt that he was about to say adieu to the scenes of his suffering. Finding that Wright had

"ESCAPE ON THE BRAIN,"

I lost no time in making what I considered the necessary preliminaries.

I first saw one of the prisoners, whom I had been told by the sergeant would be allowed to issue the potatoes. I requested him to make the issue upon receiving a certain signal from me, which I made him understand perfectly.

I then asked Lieut. Wright to step to the end of the porch, near where the corn bread lay that was intended for the rebel guard. I followed immediately after, but was observed by the sergeant, who seemed to wonder at this singular flank movement; he said nothing however, as we allayed his suspicions of our intentions, by sitting down and entering into conversation.

ESCAPING WITH RATIONS INTENDED FOR THE REBEL GUARD.

In a moment more a citizen came up and called the attention of the sergeant.

The signal was made, and the half starved men closed up for their potatoes. It was now getting dark, I hastily took possession of the corn bread, and taking advantage of the crowd which screened us from the guard, we sloped for a small clump of bushes that were but a few rods distant.

The potatoes were no sooner distributed than our absence was noticed by the guard.

The sergeant suddenly aroused himself and exclaimed, "By dog on't, the damned Yankee officers have done gone, and taken all of our corn bread. I will have them if it costs me a horse."

Calling out a corporal and four men, he instructed them to proceed to a plantation for hounds, and to bring back the Yanks either dead or alive. He thought it probable that we would take the Springfield road, as that was the nearest route to our lines.

We were all this time so near the guard that we could hear distinctly every word that was spoken, and, as a matter of course, understood the programme perfectly.

We decided with the sergeant, that the route by way of Springfield was unquestionably the one to be preferred; but we did not consider it policy to strike the road when we knew it was being patrolled with hounds, and concluded not to be in any hurry until the excitement was over.

As soon as it was sufficiently dark to warrant a move a safe expedient, we hurriedly decamped from our place of concealment, and made our way around to the Middle Ground road, over which we had passed but a few hours before under guard. We leaped across it so as to avoid the suspicion which tracks would very naturally excite, and hastened into a large swamp but a short distance from town. While there, we decided upon the course to be pursued, which was recommended by Wright.

The lieutenant has been over the Middle Ground road before, to within a few miles of Springfield, where he was re-captured; and hence his experience will be good fortune for both, as we intend to get back to Springfield as quickly as possible, and then strike for the point on the Savannah river near where I was arrested.

We remained in the swamp until after ten o'clock, when Wright started up and told me to follow. He then went in quest of an old negro hut, where we had before obtained succor. It was within a stone's throw of the plantation house, and therefore not safely approached without a thorough reconnoisance.

Secreting me in a corner of the fence, which surrounds the plantation, Wright proceeded forthwith to the hut, in which he was confident that

OLD RICHARD

slept; for this was the name of the kind hearted negro who had supplied him with hoe cake and bacon before he was re-taken at Springfield.

It required but a moment to convince Richard that his guest was none other than Massa Wright, whom he had befriended during his escape, and whom he had the mortification to see pass back toward Sylvania a prisoner in the afternoon.

I was soon introduced, with all due formality, to this swarthy descendant of Ham, whose warm and hearty shake of the hand convinced me, beyond a doubt, that he was an earnest friend to the Yankee, who would not hesitate to stake his life if necessary in an endeavor to further our wishes.

CONFIDING OUR PLANS TO A NEGRO.

Wright said that he had found a friend, and that I must make arrangements for the grub. I said to Richard, "We want to leave this place to-morrow night at twelve o'clock, and would like to take four days' rations with us. Can you let us have some bacon and sweet potatoes to put with our corn bread? He replied, "It is a pretty hard case, massa; but dis yer darky will do de best he can. Can't get nuffin on dis plantation, but recon I can buy some potatoes down at Massa Smith's, three miles from yer, and will go down there after I finish my task to-morrow."

"As to meat," he said, "you know, massa, dat in the souf de slave takes what de white folks frows away; and I recon you all could'nt eat a tainted ham dat old massa gib me tother day; but if you can, God knows dis chile gibs it to you wid all his heart."

I gave him to understand that we should be greatly obliged for the described ham; as we have become so entirely oblivious to the sense of taste that we do not stop to question the quality of anything which can be eaten by man.

CONCEALED IN AN OLD PINE TREE TOP.

The ration question being settled, we asked Richard if he could not take us to some safe spot where no rebel would ever think of coming. Leading the way, our colored friend took us to a swamp, and left us in our present place of concealment in an old pine tree top.

Here we have spent the day unmolested and unobserved by any one.

The owl and whippowil have lost no time in filling our ears with their inspiring music, and the sighing of the stately pine and cypress seem to hint that we have yet to learn our indebtedness to these dismal wilds that have concealed alike both friend and foe.

Here the rebel deserter seeks repose from the vigilant pursuit of the conscripting officer, and here too the escaped prisoner finds a favorable haunt, where he may to some extent feel secure from the searches of the hound and bushwhacker.

I had always thought that a prisoner of war was justified in making his escape, but here it is regarded a crime, and he who dares to make the attempt, is tracked like a felon or an outlaw. I cannot help asking with the poet Whittier,

> "Is this the land our fathers loved,
> The freedom which they toiled to win,
> Is this the earth whereon they moved,
> Are these the graves they slumber in?"

How wonderfully degenerated have become these unworthy descendants of the mighty fathers of the revolution. Could their spirits but speak from the heavens, they would warn these fiends of earth, not to stain the pages of history by acts so foul and barbarous, that the most unfeeling savage would shrink with horror from their contemplation.

Twenty-fifth Day.

In a Swamp, near Springfield, Ga.,
Thursday,—*December* 21.

We met old Richard last night at the spot agreed upon, near a spring on his master's plantation.

He gave us the tainted meat which had been spoken of the previous night, and a few sweet potatoes. This was the best that he could do for us, and after we had asked God to bless him for his kindness, and told him that we believed the day was not far distant, when he would be a free man, started on our way rejoicing, hoping that we might reach our lines before we should need another supply. We walked about twenty-five miles after leaving Richard, for the most part keeping the road over which we had marched while prisoners on our way to Sylvania.

Our progress was necessarily very slow, for to use a blunt expression, I was about "played out;" the result of long exposure and fatigue.

My weight at the present time cannot be more than ninety pounds.

Wright is a hardy western man, much larger and stronger than myself, and then too, he is the fortunate possessor of a very good pair of shoes, which are almost indispensable to the success of an escaped prisoner; they were given him by a negro, soon after his escape from Columbia. During the night's tramp he carried me through several swamps on his back, as I was entirely too weak to make my way along without falling into slough holes.

Nothing has yet occurred to lessen our chances for reaching Sherman, although at one time we came so near being seen by two rebel soldiers, that we had barely time to turn from the road and secrete ourselves behind a log, when they passed the spot where we had stood but a moment before.

REBEL DESERTERS.

It was a bright moonlight night, and had they been looking for Yanks, they could have found us very readily; but it appeared from their conversation that they were conscripts, and that not feeling disposed to fight against the defenders of the "old flag," they had deserted from Gen. Wheeler's command, and were making their way back to their homes in Tennessee. We did not venture to hail them, but thinking that for the alleged reasons they were justified in deserting the rebel ranks, we silently wished them success, and pushed on.

At day-break this morning we came to a halt not far from our present place of concealment, thinking that we should be perfectly secure from the haunts of men, but the dawn of day revealed to our vision a plantation house. Seeing that it was occupied showed us the impropriety of remaining longer where we were thus exposed, and we hastily got up and "dusted." Walked about half a mile, keeping clear of the road, and then stopped where we are now, secreted between the roots of some large cypress trees.

We shall remain here until dark.

The moon does not rise this evening till nearly twelve o'clock, so that it will be policy to take our tramp during the fore part of the night.

Heavy canonading in the direction of Savannah since yesterday morning.

Twenty-sixth Day.

On our way, with renewed obstacles, }
Friday,—*December* 22. }

Many are the incidents and adventures of the past twenty-four hours.

In accordance with intentions, we set off on our walk at an early hour last night. Had not proceeded far when a plantation became visible.

A PROPOSITION.

Wright said, "Glazier, if you would like a good supper and something to put in the haversack I will tell you where you can make a raise on a safe scale, by just representing yourself to be a rebel, and trusting to your face." We always considered it advisable to replenish the commissary department as often as possible; and I asked him to mention the particulars. He replied that the plantation house, toward which we were directing our eyes, was occupied by a planter's wife and some small children, whose husband and father was in the rebel army. He had also been informed that there were no hounds upon the plantation.

THE INTERVIEW WITH MRS. KEYTON.—TURNING THE TABLES.

After listening to the details, we agreed upon a signal which should warn him of my approach upon returning from the designed foraging expedition, and then I went in quest of the house.

Stepping up to the door, I rapped, and a very intelligent lady soon made her appearance.

I asked, " Can you give this rebel a supper?"

She replied, " You shall have the best the house affords;" and invited me to step in and take a seat by the fire. I did so, saying, as I took my seat, " Madam, I am shocked at the dastardly conduct of Gen. Sherman in his march through Georgia. It has been characterized by nothing but what should excite the revenge, and move to action every man possessing a true southern spirit. Our aged citizens, who have banded together for mutual protection, have been treated as bushwhackers—have been driven from their homes, and their property confiscated. Our hounds, always true to the interests of the south, have been shot down by the roadside for no other reason than because they have been used in tracking escaped prisoners"—

Here I was interrupted by the lady, who remarked, to my very great surprise, that she could not see that the Yankees were much worse than the Confederates, after all. She said:

"When the Federal army passed through the state, it took from the rich the supplies necessary for its sustenance; and when our cavalry followed on in the rear, it took nearly all that was left, seeming to care but little for our wants; often stripping defenceless women and children of their last morsel of bread."

G. I regret that the conduct of our troops has been such as to give you reasons for complaint.

Lady. I too regret that our men have not proved themselves worthy of a cause which they appear so willing to defend.

G. Remember that our commissary department has been broken up, and that we are entirely dependent upon the people for the subsistence of a large army.

L. And what do you think of present prospects?

G. Our future seems dark — our cause appears almost hopeless; but the sacrifices of our gallant dead remain unavenged. We must fight while there is a man left, and die in the last ditch.

L. If there is no longer any hope of success, I should say that it would be better to lay down our arms at once, and go back under the old flag.

G. We must fight.

L. It is wickedness to continue this awful massacre of human beings without some prospect of ultimate success.

G. Very true; but we have lost all in this struggle, and must sell our lives as dearly as possible.

L. My husband is a captain in the 25th Ga. Infantry. He is the father of these children, and is very dear to both them and me. Long have I prayed that he might be spared to return to his family, but fear that we shall never be permitted to see him again. When he entered the army I admired his patriotism, and was glad to see him go in defence of what I supposed to be the true policy of the southern people; but we have been deceived from the beginning by our military and political leaders. It is time to open our eyes, and see what obstinacy has brought us. We are conquered. Let us adhere to the administration of the Federal government ere we are ruined.

G. Madam your sympathies appear to be with the Federals.

L. It is not strange, I was born and educated in New England,— and your speech would indicate that you too are not a native of the south.

G. You are right, I am a New Yorker by birth, but have been for a long time in South Carolina.

After partaking of the frugal meal set before me, which consisted of corn bread and sweet potatoes. I thanked the lady for her kindness, and told her that I regretted very deeply that I was not in a situation to remunerate her for so much trouble. Noticing my blue pants as I arose from the table, she observed: "It is impossible for me to know our men from the Federals by the uniform, but a few days since, two soldiers asked me to get them some supper, claiming to be scouts to Gen. Wheeler; they told many very plausible stories, and the next day, to my astonishment, I was charged with harboring Yankee spies."

G. I do not wonder that you find it difficult to distinguish the Confederate from the Yankee soldier, for in these trying times a poor rebel is compelled to wear anything he can get. The dead are always stripped, and at this season of the year we find the Federal uniform far more comfortable than our own.

L. It must be an awful extremity that could tempt men to strip the dying and the dead.

G. We have become so much accustomed to such practices, that we are unmoved by scenes which might appall and sicken those who have never served in our ranks.

L. I sincerely hope that these murderous practices will soon be at an end.

G. I must go madam; may I know to whom I am so much indebted for my supper and kind entertainment this evening?

L. Mrs. James Keyton,—and what may I call your name?

G. Willard Glazier, 53d Alabama Mounted Infantry.

L. Should you chance to meet the 25th Ga., please enquire for Capt. Keyton, and say to him that his wife and children are well and send their love.

G. He shall certainly have your message if

it is my good fortune to find him out. Good night.

The interview with Mrs. Keyton ended, which seemed to convince her that I was a bitter rebel. I hastened out to receive the congratulations of Wright upon my success, but found him in very bad humor, as he was entirely out of patience with waiting for my return. I explained to him the reason of the delay, but all to no purpose, for he was so provoked that he would not listen, and thus feeling a little angry at each other, we moved toward Springfield. Being determined to gain as much information as possible concerning the strength and movements of the enemy in General Sherman's rear, we made a thorough reconnoisance before leaving Springfield.

We found General Iverson's head quarters to be at that place, and was at one time within fifteen paces of the house which he occupied.

We were so near his provost guard, as to hear distinctly every word that was spoken. They were discussing present prospects, and the news which they had received yesterday of the fall of Savannah. It seemed to be the prevailing opinion that the Confederate army was about played out, and that sooner or later

ILL FATED DIXIE

would be compelled to submit to the tyranical rule of the invader. One long, gaunt looking fellow, who appeared to be the mouth piece for a large number, straightened himself up in front of a fire, around which a group had gathered, and burst forth as follows: "By dog on't, the damned blue bellies have got ahead of weuns on this tramp." I could not help thinking what a change had taken place in their views since the 17th, when we were prisoners at Wheeler's head quarters, for at that time they asserted that they had

GEN. SHERMAN JUST WHERE THEY WANTED HIM.

Now their victim is evidently in the ascendant, and the army that was to sacrifice its chivalrous blood in the defences of Savannah, seeks safety in flight, having abandoned its artillery and supplies. Leaving Springfield, it was the intention to strike the Savannah river road at Helmy, where we supposed the enemy's outpost to be. My companion knew nothing about this route, and left all to me, as I had been recaptured near that point. It is by no means an easy task to pursue any desired course in this swampy country, intersected as it is by blind roads. The sun, moon and stars are our only guides; and it is to them that we are chiefly indebted for our success since the escape from Sylvania.

While in South Carolina and Northern Georgia we depended entirely upon the negroes for guidance; but the passage of our army through this section of the state opened the way to freedom, and invited the bondman to cast off his shackels, and enjoy the blessings of liberty.

Strange as it may seem, nearly every slave has embraced the opportunity presented him, and has very quietly taken leave of his kind old master without waiting for ceremony. I say strange, for the simple reason that it has been the boast of the southerner, that the slave would not exchange his chains for freedom; that he was happy when governed by a kind master, and would not seek to better his condition by a change.

Having passed Springfield about six miles we found day-light approaching, and hurriedly turned from the road which we had been following for more than an hour, and secreted ourselves in some tall swamp grass. Here we laid little more than an hour, when we were suddenly

STARTLED BY THE YELPING OF HOUNDS.

Wright turned to me and said, "We are followed."

I asked, "What do you propose to do?"

W. I am undecided.

G. There is no time for reflection. If we are not off at once, we will be prisoners before leaving this swamp.

W. Well, off it is then; and jumping into our shoes, which we had taken off in order to dry our feet, we got out of the swamp in double quick time, crossed the road, and, taking the sun for a guide, struck a southeasterly course, leaping fences and ditches, fording streams, and passing through thickets, that would greatly retard the progress of the

BUSHWHACKERS IN PURSUIT.

The chase continued until about one o'clock. The hounds, for the most part, being so near that we could hear their yelping distinctly, when, fortunately, we came to a large creek; jumping into the stream, we followed the current fifty or sixty rods, and then, turning to the sun for our point of compass, pushed on.

The precaution taken upon our arrival at the creek must have foiled the hounds; for we had not proceeded far when we became fully satisfied that we had out-generaled the bushwhackers. We did not halt, however, but continued on toward the promised land. Greatly encouraged by our success since morning, we became so indiscreet and reckless as to venture into open fields whenever they happened to be on our line of march.

A NARROW ESCAPE.

At about two o'clock P. M., just as we were clearing the outskirts of a swamp, I was surprised to see my companion drop suddenly behind a large cypress tree without uttering a word. I followed his example, not deeming it prudent to ask a question.

I fixed my attention upon Wright, who, after remaining motionless a few moments, raised his head and looked to the front. Falling back behind the aged cypress, he whispered, "Did you see the picket?" I answered, "No;" but looking up, saw that we were within twenty rods of armed men.

No further observations were necessary to convince us that the sooner out of such quarters the better. We had not time to move, however, ere a cavalry patrol came up to visit the post, and to give new instructions. As soon as the patrol had passed, we crawled back upon our hands and knees into the swamp, keeping behind a clump of large trees that screened us from the picket. Coming to a dry spot, we halted to consider the propriety of proceeding farther, as there was great danger of being seen in an attempt to leave that place.

Wright decided that it would be policy to remain where we were, and here a difference of opinion arose again; as I was so wet and cold that the thought of confining myself to such limited quarters, I confess, made me not a little uneasy; for we could neither stand up nor lie down. Our clothes, too, were wet, the weather extremely cold, and we had not slept in forty-eight hours; and then, too, the idea of sitting up like a pair of mummies five hours. I told my companion that there was no such thing in the book, and that I would strike for dry land if it cost me a re-capture.

Wright said that he would not move, and I set off on my own hook.

I passed the doubtful point by watching the

picket, and making good time when their backs were turned.

Getting out of the swamp, I went in quest of a favorable haunt where I might lay my weary limbs and dry my clothes.

I was delighted as well as amused to find W. close upon my heels, glad enough to abandon the sitting posture for something more agreeable. I welcomed him to my new place of concealment; and here we have spent the afternoon unmolested by any one.

Our distance from the picket is not more than eighty rods. We are inclined to think it the outpost.

AN AMUSING INCIDENT

occurred this evening a few moments after sunset. The weather being extremely cold, and our clothes still damp, we agreed that a small fire would be very pleasant; and, suiting the action to the thought, dug a hole in the ground, gathered some pine knots and started a blaze, which in my judgment could not have been seen by any one at a distance of fifty feet, but, to my companion, it appeared to be of gigantic proportions; and his imagination became so much excited that he set one of his feet over it, and thus put an end to my enjoyment as well as the fire.

Twenty-seventh Day.

Head Quarters, 10th Iowa Vols., Savannah, Ga.,
Saturday,— *December* 23.

This is the happiest day of my life; and one which will ever remain a bright landmark in my recollections of the past.

We succeeded in flanking the picket last night just after dark, and was not long in finding a colored friend, familiarly known as Uncle Philip, among his acquaintances, who informed us that we had passed the outpost.

Our joy was inexpressible, and our emotions beyond control; for more glorious news never fell upon the ear.

Uncle Philip also informed us that our friends were at Cherokee Hill, on the Savannah River road, only eight miles distant. We asked him if he could not guide us to the lines. He replied "Ize neber been down dah, massa, since Mr. Sherman's company went to Savannah; but I reckon you can get Mr. Jones, a free colored man, to take you ober. He is a mighty bright pusson, and understands de swamps jest like a book." Calling at Mr. Jones's hut, we learned from his wife that he was out on a scout, but would be in by eleven o'clock. She assured us that he was ever glad to do all in his power for the Yankees, and asked us to come into the hut and await his return. We very reluctantly complied with her invitation, fearing that

REBEL SCOUTS

might venture down between the lines, and thus blast our brilliant prospects.

Mrs. Jones, however, was by no means a dull tactician, and offered her two sons, one a lad of eight, and the other six years, for outpost duty.

I divided the command and posted the pickets, stationing the oldest boy in the road, at a distance of twenty rods from the hut, and used the other for patrol, who was to keep a sharp lookout; and in case any one might be seen approaching the post, was to notify his mother, thereby giving her an opportunity to conceal us.

This matter attended to, a generous supply of hoe cake and parched corn delighted our eyes; for Auntie was not long in appeasing our hunger with the best her humble cot afforded.

Jones came in at the mentioned hour, but did not think himself sufficiently well acquainted with the safest route to warrant his acting in the capacity of guide; but, like all other negroes that I have met in the south, he very readily called to mind one whom he thought would accompany us, and whom he could recommend very highly as an active and intelligent fellow.

EFFORTS TO OBTAIN A GUIDE.

Securing a small piece of fat pine for a torch to light our way through an intervening swamp, we started for the Savannah river road, beyond which the negro could be found, whose many good qualities had been pointed out to myself and companion. Much to our astonishment,

COLORED MAN NO. 3

was not so well posted as had been affirmed; but, luckily, and much to our delight, he very promptly referred to another negro who had come up from the lines since morning, and whom he knew would be glad to return with us. The negro last recommended bore the name of

MARCH DASHER.

We found him to be a genuine Ethiopian, as black as any colored individual I have ever met; and as dignified and devout as he was active and swarthy. Upon being asked if he could show us the way to Cherokee Hill, replied,

"I'LL DO IT, MASSA, IF GOD BE MY HELPER."

We desired to start at once, but could not persuade him to move before day-light. He said, "Dis chile knows where de pickets is in de day time, but knows nuffin 'bout 'em after dark." Several attempts were made to induce us to remain in the hut till morning; but no amount of safety insurances could persuade us to take such an apparently inconsiderate step.

The idea that it would not be policy to move on before morning inclined us to think that our landlord might be treacherous, and we were not a little

UNEASY UNTIL PRAYER WAS OFFERED FOR OUR BENEFIT,

when we became fully satisfied that we could at least repose confidence in his fidelity. As soon as prayers were concluded, we betook ourselves to a pine thicket, determined to give March no peace until he should set off with us.

THE NEGRO'S CLOCK NEEDS NO REPAIRING.

At about one o'clock in the morning, Wright turned out and told him that day had just began to break. He got up, came to the door, looked for the seven stars, and then remarked, in a very good humored way, "I recon it's good many hours yet till break ob day, massa. Yer can't fool March on de time; his clock neber breaks down. It's jest right ebery time." Feeling somewhat chagrined at his ill success, W. returned to the thicket saying, "Glazier, there is no use of being in a sweat; for you might as well undertake to move a mountain as to get the start of that colored individual." We made no further attempt to dupe our guide, but very impatiently awaited his call. He came to our place of concealment at the first peep of day, and said

"GEMMEN, NOW IZE READY

to take you right plum into Mr. Sherman's company by 'sun up.'" We followed him without ceremony; and just as old sol began to tint the hill-sides with his first rays, we saw, with unbounded joy,

A GROUP OF BLUE COATS

watching very eagerly our approach; for it was the outpost. At first, we were evidently regarded as an enemy; but by taking off our hats and making friendly signs, their suspicions were allayed, and they beckoned us to come on. A most cordial reception was given us by the picket, which proved to be a detail from the 101 Illinois Volunteers, 20th Army Corps.

We took each man by the hand, congratulating him upon his good fortune in surviving the death-blow to rebellion in Georgia; and they in return rejoiced at our successful escape. Haversacks were opened, and placed at our disposal. There was a great demand for hard tack and coffee; but the beauty of it all was,

MAJ. TURNER WAS NOT THERE,

to say what he has often repeated, "Reduce their rations; I'll teach the damned scoundrels not to attempt an escape." I shall ever remember my feelings when I began to realize the fact that I was no longer a prisoner, and when I beheld the old flag floating triumphantly over the invincible veterans that followed the Great General down to the sea.

CHAPTER XII.

Head Quarters, 10th Iowa Volunteers, Savannah, Ga.,—*December* 24, 1864.

After breakfast yesterday morning, at the picket post, we came into the city with a brigade of the 20th Army Corps, which formed a part of the rear guard of Gen. Sherman's Army.

It would have been a difficult matter to have identified us in our motley uniform. For myself, I was clad in a coat of southern gray, blue pants, my shoes—before described—a bewitched looking hat and gray blanket, which for months had answered the purpose of bed and bedding.

My haversack was a curiosity in its way, being composed of an old towel, which was sewed up by Lemon many weeks before. Said haversack had borne its journey well, but now showed unmistakable signs of dissolution. Sweet potatoes, unless of a fabulous size, slipped through as readily as money through a soldier's fingers;

and large must be the loaf which could find a resting place within its awful depths.

Many pleasant-incidents occurred during our ride into the city.

A major and surgeon, whose names I failed to learn, kindly offered us their horses, and dismounted for our convenience. The offer was gratefully accepted, for we were both weak and weary, and Lieut. Wright had assisted me for some time on our way.

On reaching the city, Wright's first inquiry was for his old regiment; but it was like a search in the dark. The unsettled state of the army rendered it difficult to learn the location of any particular regiment or brigade; but we found the corps to which his regiment belongs, and were sent, under guard, from corps to regimental head-quarters, with a demand for recognition, and a receipt therefor.

Such treatment seemed hard at first; but when we reflected upon our checkered costume, and suspicious appearance, we readily fell into their way of thinking; for, until we were identified, it would have been no wonder that we were looked upon as spies or desperadoes. So, submitting with the best grace at our disposal, we were soon

PRONOUNCED GENUINE UNION SOLDIERS.

To-night we are stopping with Capt. A. L. Swallow, who commands the lieutenant's company. He is a noble man, and has administered to our wants like a father. Our circumstances being known, no pains are spared in making us comfortable and happy. This morning I was presented with a fine pair of pants, a pair of boots, and under clothing. It is delightful to be once more where we are not watched and hunted like felons, and to look upon the faces of friends.

Captain Swallow took up a contribution for my especial benefit to-day, to which the officers of his regiment contributed generously.

This afternoon we witnessed the review of the 12th Army Corps by Gen. Sherman; it was grand, and the whole army are devoted to their leader.

Christmas Day.

The greater part of this day has been spent in the city. Took dinner with Mr. H. Brown. His residence is on Congress street, opposite the Pulaski House, Mr. B. is known as a firm Union man, and although he has suffered much from adherence to his principles, and frequently been stripped of all his goods, he still remains true to the old flag and the government of his fathers.

Lieut. E. H. Fales, who was a fellow prisoner at Charleston, was found secreted at Mr. Brown's house when our army entered Savannah. The lieutenant was in the city for more than a month, representing himself as a very innocent foreigner, but was at one time conscripted and ordered on the defences.

At Kilpatrick's Head Quarters, on the Ogeechee River,—*Dec.* 26.

Lieut. F. and myself obtained horses at the quartermaster's of the 20th Corps, and rode out here this afternoon. My object here is to be identified by Kilpatrick, in order to secure transportation north, as he is the only officer in the Department who knew me to be in the United States' service previous to my capture. The general has had the kindness to furnish me with the necessary papers, and I shall return to Savannah in the morning, to go north by the first boat.

We took supper with the general and Capt. Estice of his staff, who were much interested in my accounts of prison life and escapes. One hardly likes to be the hero of his own tales, yet I love to dwell upon them, and the goodness of God which accompanied us all the way.

My term of service has expired, and I long once more to behold the faces of the dear ones at home. This afternoon I returned to Savannah, and had, in addition to my other Christmas gifts, a good vest and change of linen. They were presented by Capt. Estice, and render me quite human in appearance.

I had hoped to leave Savannah before this, but the army is in an unsettled state, and I must bide my time.

There is great suffering among the poorer classes here, it being difficult to obtain even the very necessaries of life.

Steamship Planter, near Savannah, Ga.,— *December* 29.

This is the boat which was run out of Charleston Harbor by a negro pilot, who now commands her under the title of captain. The craft has seen hard service, and was badly peppered upon her retirement from rebel service.

She is now in government employ, and runs as far as the obstructions in the river, and returns the following day. She is met by boats at the end of her route, transfers her cargo, and returns for another load.

Lieut. Fales will accompany me to New York. Wright would have accompanied me, but his term of service having expired, he waits to be mustered out before leaving Savannah.

Steamship Ashland, Hilton Head, South Carolina,—*December* 30.

We were transferred from the Planter to the Delaware during the night, and came on the latter boat to this place, where I am ticketed for the Empire State. Bless her dear old name! How many a poor fellow, who started out with me, will never again press her soil, nor be welcomed home by those who await their coming. We expect to reach New York in four or five days. The Ashland is a small ocean steamer, and is commanded by Thomas Cowdry, an old sea captain, weatherbeaten and brave. The weather is cold and windy, and the little craft rolls fearfully.

In a Gale, off Cape Hatteras,—*January* 2, 1865.

Yesterday we were in a fearful gale, which threatened us with a speedy and watery grave.

All the passengers were sea-sick, and all of the crew, save those directly connected with the management of the vessel. This being my first experience with old Neptune, my case was none of the mildest. The captain comforts us with the strength of his ship, and points out her beauties in a way quite mystifying to a landsman. He assures us of a speedy calm, and a delightful trip. May his prophecies prove correct.

This is a remarkable new year to me. Just out of prison, army, and a strange land, I am tossing on the sea like a homeless wanderer, and only wait to see the shores of my own state. Once there, I shall rest on my laurels until health and strength are regained, when I may go out again—not, I trust, for the defence of my country, but to look upon a land resting in the calm serenity of freedom and power.

Jan. 4. Our boat grated upon the wharf late last night, and I soon awoke to the realization that I was breathing the air of New York. Our voyage has been pleasant and full of adventure. The passengers, taking pity upon the poor stranger boy, made me a generous purse of thirty dollars, which was presented by a fellow officer—Lieut. Col. Alexander, of an Ohio regiment.

I hope soon to be snugly settled in my father's house; till then, dear reader adieu.

"Now our prison life is over! Ah! it is a pleasant thought,
  And we here await our furloughs, ere again our homes are sought.
Farewell South, and all thy dead lines! Farewell traitors, robbers too!
Cherished friends of youth and childhood, we are coming home to you!
And will not your smiles of welcome half repay our griefs and cares,
When once more you see us sitting in the old familiar chairs?
But there's One who reigns above us — we should give our thanks to Him,
For the bright hopes in the bosoms, where sweet hope alas was dim.
For His kind and loving presence, that at last we lived to stand
Free from prison life in Dixie, in our own beloved and loyal land
Let us pray for peace forever, for the Union glad and free,
With a tear for comrades faithful, whom we never more shall see.
Ever trusting One above us, though the clouds may gather fast,
Knowing well our Father's mansion will receive us at the last."

CHAPTER XIII.

The succeeding pages are devoted principally to the testimony of individuals who have been confined in other prisons.

AT MILLIN.

Conspicuous upon the list of rebel prisons stands the pen, known south as Camp Lawton, near Millin, Georgia.

The following is the testimony of Serg't. W. Goodyear, 7th Regiment, C. V., who was removed to that place from Andersonville on the 1st of November, 1864.

It was pleasantly situated, about eighty miles north of Savannah, in a country where pine forests abound. Indeed, these were a prominent feature in the external surroundings of many of the southern prisons. Trees would be felled, a clearing made, and here located the rude structure that was to be the cheerless home of thousands for long, weary months. Could a voice be given to these silent groves, and they become witnesses of what they have seen and heard, what revelations would be made of things that can never be known now!

The medium of human language fails to convey all the meaning involved in prison life in the south. It is true that a great part of the suffering in this present war, as in all wars, must forever remain with the secrets of *unwritten history*. A few, who were themselves actors in the tragic scenes, may rehearse the story of their individual experience, and thus furnish, as it were, a key to unlock the gates through which others may enter and take a look. This is the only way in which the people at large can become acquainted with this thrilling portion of the war; and authentic and reliable statements are therefore of deep interest and importance.

Forty-four acres of ground were inclosed by the stockade at Millin. The large pine timber, which was cut down at the commencement of operations for building the prison, was left upon the ground; and when the first prisoners went into their confinement there, they found these to be greatly to their advantage; for they were able to construct for themselves comfortable huts of the logs and branches lying about them. In this respect they were more fortunate than many, or most others. The last division that entered had no shelter at all, or at least of any account. A small stream of good water ran through the centre, which the men highly prized, particularly as it afforded the much needed privilege of bathing. At the time of my arrival there, the list of prisoners numbered nine thousand. The weather was very cold and stormy; and as the majority of the men were very poorly clad, many of them being without shoes, blankets or coats, and also without shelter, the suffering was very great. No medicine was issued to the men within the stockade, and but very few were taken outside to the hospital; consequently the mortality was fearful. The number of deaths averaged from twenty-five to thirty-five per day. The prevailing diseases were such as are common to almost all prisons—the scurvy, diarrhœa and rheumatism. It was no uncommon occurrence for the morning light to reveal the pallid faces of three or four prisoners who had laid down side by side, showing that death had claimed them all during the night. Such sights were heartrending to the most unfeeling—the most stoical. The prisoner is condemned to these things, and there is no alternative but for him to gaze upon them, however sad and revolting they may be. He must steel himself against that which once would have sent sympathy through his whole being—a gushing tide. It could not be that the fountain of pity be stirred to its depths so often. Nature could not sustain the pressure; therefore it seems that the whole is something like a martyr process, in which the very juices of life are crushed out by an uncontrollable force.

At the beginning of my stay at Millin, the rations which were issued were double the amount we had at Andersonville. We drew one pint of meal, six ounces of uncooked beef, six spoonsfull of rice, one tea-spoonful of salt, as our allowance for twenty-four hours. Beans were sometimes substituted for rice; but these were so much eaten by insects that they were often thrown away without being tasted. After a little while, however, the quantity decreased every day, so that they became nearly as small and poor as those issued in other prisons.

The prospect of being exchanged or paroled was so small that some availed themselves of the opportunity to take the oath of allegiance to the Confederate government, and entered the rebel service. The inducements which were offered them to do this, were three bushels of sweet potatoes, a suit of clothes and one hundred dollars in Confederate scrip. I was myself acquainted with quite a number who did this; and although I would make no excuse for them, I know the motive by which they were actuated. They knew no chance of getting out of prison alive. They had barely clothes to cover their nakedness, and they thought to prolong their existence in this way; and coupled with this was the idea of escaping and fleeing to the Union lines at the very first opportunity. But the whole thing was considered a mean, disgraceful act by every true patriot. I would have died a dozen deaths rather than to have been guilty of such a thing, and there were thousands of others of the same mind.

As the time of the presidential election drew near, the rebels expressed a desire that we should vote upon the question ourselves. Accordingly ballot boxes were procured, and on the day when the people of the north were deciding the momentous issue, we gathered together in Millin Prison, and in the midst of great excitement, gave expression to our political preferences. We knew that it was *war* or

CAME TOO NEAR THE DEAD LINE.

peace. As we deposited our votes, so did we speak for one or the other, and show forth our position in the country's cause.

At sunset the votes were counted, and the result was 3,014 votes for Lincoln, and 1,050 for McClellan.

CAME TOO NEAR THE DEAD LINE.

I am indebted to O. R. Dahl, late lieutenant 15th Wisconsin Infantry, for the following particulars relative to the murder of Lieut. Turbayne, which occurred after my escape from Columbia.

On the morning of the first of December, 1864, at Camp Sorghum, about ten o'clock, the camp was startled with the report of a musket, and soon the report spread through camp that Lieut. Turbayne, 68th New York, had been *shot*— murdered by the guard, a Mr. Williams, of Newbury Court House, S. C.

Turbayne was walking along a path that ran by the corner of a hut, near the dead line, but *inside of it.*

Along this path the prisoners had walked hundreds of times without fear, for it was on our own ground. As Turbayne came along, the guard brought his piece to the shoulder, halted, and ordered him back. He turned to go, walked a step or two, when the villain shot him through the back, the ball passing through his lungs. He staggered a few steps, fell, and died within a few minutes.

Not only did Major Griswold refuse to investigate the matter, but after the murderer had been relieved by the officer of the day, he sent him back on duty that afternoon on the front line, and also into camp the next morning, surrounded by a body guard, for fear the officers would do violence to him — an insult of the blackest dye.

CHAPTER XIV.

SALISBURY PENITENTIARY.

The prison at Salisbury, North Carolina, which became so notorious during the war as one of the most loathsome dungeons in rebeldom, was at first intended as a place of punishment for southern soldiers guilty of military offences, and as a place of committal for hostages, who were usually sentenced to hard labor. It more recently came into general use, and hundreds of unfortunate victims said their last farewell in that miserable den. In order that we may obtain a better view of this horrible abode, I will transcribe the testimony of Messrs. Richardson and Brown, both widely known as correspondents for the public press.

The following statement was made by the former, before the Committee on the Conduct of the War:

I was captured on a hay bale in the Mississippi river, opposite Vicksburg, on the 3d of

May, 1863, at midnight. After a varied experience in six different prisons, I was sent to Salisbury on the 3d of February, 1864, from which place I escaped on the 18th of December following.

For months, Salisbury was the most endurable prison I had seen; there were 600 inmates. They were exercised in the open air, comparatively well fed, and kindly treated. Early in October, 10,000 regular prisoners of war arrived. It immediately changed into a scene of cruelty and horror; it was densely crowded, rations were cut down and issued very irregularly; friends outside could not even send in a plate of food.

The prisoners suffered considerably, and often intensely, for the want of bread and shelter; those who had to live or die on prison rations, always suffered from hunger; very frequently, one or more divisions of 1,000 men would receive no rations for twenty-four hours; sometimes they were without food for forty-eight hours. A few who had money would pay from five to twenty dollars in rebel currency for a little loaf of bread. Many, though the weather was inclement and snow frequent, sold the coats from their backs and shoes from their feet.

I was assured, on authority entirely trustworthy, that a great commissary warehouse near the prison was filled with provisions. The commissary found it difficult to find storage for his corn and meal; and when a subordinate asked the post commandant, Maj. John H. Gee, "Shall I give the prisoners full rations?" he replied with an oath, "No! give them quarter rations."

I know from personal observation, that corn and pork are very abundant in the region about Salisbury.

For weeks the prisoners had no shelter whatever; they were all thinly clad, thousands were barefooted, not one in twenty had an overcoat or blanket, many hundreds were without shirts, and hundreds were without blouses. One Sibley tent and one A tent were furnished to each squad of 100; with the closest crowding, these sheltered about half the prisoners. The rest burrowed in the ground, crept under the buildings, or shivered through the night in the open air upon the frozen ground.

If the rebels, at the time of our capture, had not stolen our shelter-tents, blankets, clothing and money, they would have suffered little from cold. If the prison authorities had permitted them, either on parole or under guard, to cut logs within two miles of the prison, the men would have built comfortable and ample barracks in one week; but the commandant would not consent,— he did not even furnish one-half the fuel needed.

The hospitals were in a horrible condition. More than half who entered them died in a few days. The deceased, always without coffins, were loaded into the dead-carts, piled on each other like logs of wood, and so driven out to be thrown in a trench and covered with earth.

The rebel surgeons were generally humane and attentive, and endeavored to improve the shocking condition of the hospitals; but the Salisbury and Richmond authorities disregarded their protests.

On the 25th of November, many of the prisoners had been without food for forty-eight hours, and were desperate, without any matured plan. A few of them said, "We may as well die in one way as another; let us break out of this horrible place." Some of them wrested the guns from a relief of fifteen rebel soldiers, just entering the yard, killing two who resisted, and wounding five or six others, and attempted to open the fence; but they had neither adequate tools or concert of action. Before they could effect a breach, every gun of the garrison was turned on them. The field pieces opened with grape and canister, and they dispersed to their quarters. In five minutes from its beginning the attempt was quelled, and hardly a prisoner was to be seen in the yard. The rebels killed sixteen in all, and wounded sixty. Not one-tenth of the prisoners had taken part in the attempt; and many of them were ignorant of it until they heard the guns. Deliberate, cold-blooded murders of peaceable men, where there was no pretense that they were breaking any prison regulation, were very frequent.

Our lives were never safe for one moment. Any sentinel, at any hour of the day or night, could deliberately shoot down any prisoner, or fire into a group of them, black or white, and never be taken off his post for it.

I left about 6,500 remaining in garrison on the day of my escape, and they were then dying at the average rate of twenty-eight per day, or thirteen per cent a month. The simple truth is, that the rebel authorities are murdering our soldiers at Salisbury by cold and hunger, while they might easily supply them with ample food and fuel. They are doing this systematically, and I believe are killing them intentionally, for the purpose either of forcing our government to an exchange, or forcing our men into their own army.

The testimony of Mr. Brown, also a correspondent of the *Tribune*, corroborates the above statements of Mr. Richardson. He says:

I have often wished that I could obtain a photograph of that room in Salisbury Prison; for I can give no idea of its repulsiveness and superlative squalor.

The prison was formerly a cotton factory, about ninety by thirty feet; and when we were there, they had only six or seven hundred confined within its walls. A dirtier, smokier, drearier, and more unwholsome place I had never seen than the room in which we were placed. It reminded me of some old junk-shop in South street of the city I had left, and was hung round with filthy rags, tattered quilts and blankets, reeking with vermin, which the wretched inmates used as clothes and bed covering, and thronged mostly with northern and southern citizens, most of whom were in garments long worn out, and as far removed from cleanliness as the wearers from happiness. In that abhored abode we were compelled to eat and sleep as best we might. There were but two stoves, both old and broken, in the room; and they gave out no heat, but any quantity of smoke, which filled the apartment with bitter blueness. Vermin swarmed everywhere; they tortured us while we tried to sleep on our coarse blankets, and kept us in torment when awake. No light of any kind was furnished us; and there we sat night after night in the thick darkness, inhaling the foul vapors and the acrid smoke, longing for the morning, when we could again catch a glimpse of the overarching sky.

Think of this death-life month after month! Think of men of delicate organization, accustomed to ease and luxury, of fine taste, and a passionate love for the beautiful, without a word of sympathy, or a whisper of hope, wearing their days out amid such scenes. Not a pleasant sound, nor a sweet odor, nor a vision of fairness, ever reached them. They were buried as completely as if they lay beneath the ruins of Pompeii or Herculaneum. They breathed mechanically, but were shut out from all that renders existence endurable. Every sense was shocked perpetually, and yet the heart, by a strange inconsistency, kept up its throbs, and preserved the physical being of a hundred and fifty wretched captives, who, no doubt, often prayed to die. Few persons can have any idea of a long imprisonment in the south. They usually regard it as an absence of freedom, a deprivation of the pleasures and excitements of ordinary life. They do not take into consideration the scant and miserable rations that no one, unless he be half famished, can eat; the necessity of going cold and hungry in the wet and wintry season; the constant torture from vermin, of which no care or caution can free one; the total isolation; the supreme dreariness, the dreadful monotony, the perpetual turning inward of the mind upon itself, the self-devouring of the heart, week after week, month after month, and year after year.

CHAPTER XV.

AT ANDERSONVILLE.

By Ira E. Forbes, 16th Conn. Volunteers.

It is from no unfair motives that I am induced to make the following statement of what I saw and experienced while a prisoner in the hands of the rebels during the spring, summer and autumn of 1864. I have tried to give a truthful account of some of the cruelties and sufferings which our poor boys were called to endure in filthy, loathsome southern prisons and hospitals. It seems to me there can be no reason for any one to make a false report of the miseries we received at the hands of our heartless captors and brutal prison keepers. To tell the truth of them, is all that is needed to convince any reasonable man of their barbarities and fiendish attempt to deprive our soldiers, whom the fortune of war had thrown into their power, of every comfort and enjoyment of life.

But to my narrative. I was captured April 2d, 1864, at Plymouth, North Carolina. It is to the credit of the rebel soldiers, whose good fortune it was to capture our command, stationed there to hold and defend the place, that we were treated with considerable courtesy and kindness while in their power.

To my knowledge, no outrages were committed upon any of our white troops, though I believe the small negro force with us fared very hard.

Our men were allowed to retain their blankets and overcoats, and all little articles of value which they might have upon their persons. Many of the men had about them large sums of money, which they were allowed to keep.

From Plymouth a long and wearisome march was made to Tarboro'; a very pretty town, situated on the Neuse, a few miles from Goldsboro'. By the time we arrived there the men were much fagged and worn out. The last day of the march we were without rations, and suffered a great deal from hunger and weariness. Soon after reaching our camping ground, near the town, rations were issued to us. There were a few cow peas, or beans, more properly, some corn meal, a small piece of bacon, and a very meagre allowance of salt, for each man. Some old iron kettles, tins, etc., were provided for us to cook our food in, and a small quantity of wood furnished; and we managed to prepare a repast which was very palatable to our well whetted appetites. A system of trading was immediately commenced, which was carried on for a while very briskly, but was finally prohibited by the rebel authorities.

Our men would barter away their watches, rings, gold pen-holders, pocket-knives, coat-buttons, etc., for Confederate pone cakes, hard bread, and bacon from the rebels. The most exorbitant prices were demanded by both parties; our men, however, generally getting the best bargain. We had remained at Tarboro' but a few days when orders were received to remove all the Union prisoners who could travel to Andersonville, Ga., immediately. We had already suffered much, both from hunger and exposure. Many were sick and feeble. All were anxious to leave, and we felt much relief at hearing that preparations had been made to remove us to a pleasanter and more fruitful portion of the Confederacy. We were informed that Camp Sumter, the prison to which we were going, occupied a delightful locality, and also that our food there would be more wholesome and plenteous than that which we had yet received. Their fair accounts and pleasing stories but increased our anxiety to be off; and it was with no little pleasure that, on the morning of April 29th, we bade adieu to the gloomy field into which we had been turned as so many brutes, and marched with quite joyous hearts to the depôt in town. Here we were confined, crowded by forties into small and loathsome box-cars. Besides our own enormous numbers, six rebel guards were stationed in each carriage; a name which I heard applied by a foppish young officer to the miserable concern aboard which we were literally packed. Of course, the rebels occupied the doors, and we nearly suffocated. Under such circumstances, many of the boys, less sanguine and hopeful than others, began to express doubts concerning the stories which we had heard; and intimated that they were all mere fabrications to deceive us, and make it an easier matter to convey us to Camp Sumter.

Without doubt such was the case. It is certain that they made the utmost efforts to get us through to the stockade at Andersonville under as small a guard as possible. We arrived in Charleston on Sunday morning, May 1st. To our great surprise, we found that some of the inhabitants of the city were friendly to us. They distributed tobacco and cigars among the men, and some secretly brought them food. Months afterwards, some of our suffering, dying boys found inestimable friends in the Sisters of Charity, who abode in the city.

Leaving Charleston at an early hour in the afternoon, we were hurried on at quite a rapid rate toward Savannah, Georgia. About six o'clock in the evening it commenced storming very hard, and, being on platform cars, we were thoroughly drenched with rain.

At about nine o'clock we changed cars a short distance from Savannah for Macon, at which place we arrived the following day a little past noon.

I was much pleased with Macon. It is a handsome city, and pleasantly situated on the Ocmulgee river — a stream of some importance. It contained a number of fine residences, several churches, two or three large iron foundries, and a car-factory, I believe. Trees, flowers, and gardens presented an appearance not unlike that of early summer at home. Almost everything there was looking pleasant and beautiful, and I felt very sad at leaving, knowing, as I then did, something of the true character of our future abode.

Late in the afternoon of May 2d we left Macon on our way to Andersonville, at which place we arrived some time in the evening. Soon after our arrival there, we were marched into an open field near by, where we remained during the night. It being very cold, large fires had been made by the rebel soldiers for our comfort. For this little act of kindness we indeed felt very grateful to them. The next morning, May 3d, a sinister-looking little foreigner came down to us, and, with considerable bluster and many oaths, began to form us into detachments, containing 270 men each. These detachments were subdivided into messes of ninety each, and placed under the control of a sergeant, whose duty it was to attend roll call, drawing rations, etc. At length, everything being ready, we were escorted into the prison under a strong guard. It is impossible to describe our feelings at this time. Everywhere around us were men in the most abject wretchedness and misery. Immediately on our arrival among them they began to gather around us, and, in a very touching manner, related the sad story of their sufferings and wrongs. We could only sympathize with them. Beyond that, we could do nothing. We knew full well that the same cruelties which they had experienced were in store for us. The prospect before us was dark indeed. In the afternoon of the day on which I entered the prison, I ventured out some distance into the camp. Everywhere was the most unmistakable evidence of intense suffering and destitution. Hundreds of the men were without shelter, and but very few had any comfortable clothing.

The supply of wood was very small — scarcely enough to cook with; and the poor fellows were obliged to lie, night after night, week after week, on the cold, damp ground, without even a fire to warm themselves by.

The rebels may claim that there was some cause for not issuing a sufficient quantity of food to our prisoners at Andersonville; but for not granting us wood enough to keep us warm, and to cook with, there can be no apology. On three sides of the prison there was an immense woodland, from which all the wood that we needed could have been provided with very little difficulty. The same holds true in regard to shelter. I am persuaded that it was an act of premeditated inhumanity on the part of our enemies not to give us shelter. It would have required but a few weeks' time, and a few scores of hands, to have built barracks for our comfortless boys there, which would have been the means of saving hundreds of precious lives. If the rebels would have granted us even the rough, unhewn logs, and axes to work with, we would have built them ourselves.

The camp at this time was in a most loathsome condition. It then covered an area of about fifteen acres, and was inclosed by a high stockade, built of pine logs, hewn and closely joined together.

Upward of twenty feet from the stockade was the fatal "dead line," beyond which any poor fellow passing was almost certain to be fired upon by some of the ever watchful sentries. In the centre of the camp, and extending entirely around it, was a broad ravine, which, toward the beginning of summer, became one of the filthiest places imaginable, and was one of the chief causes of the vast amount of sickness which existed during the months of July and August following. About this time, May 10th, the average rate of mortality daily, was upward of fifteen. It afterward rose as high as seventy-five and one hundred.

Sunday morning, June 19th, one of our men, unfortunately getting beyond the dead line, was fired upon by the guard. He was missed, but the ball wounded two others, one severely.

On the 21st, another man was shot while merely reaching beyond the dead line for a small piece of wood which he needed.

Toward the close of June, sickness and death began to prevail in camp to an alarming extent. The men died by scores daily. But few were admitted to the hospital, and even when received there, it was not until life was nearly extinct. The old prisoners who had been incarcerated for months at Belle Island were falling away with fearful rapidity. Nearly all of those still living, could see nothing before them but a slow, torturing death, from a most painful disease, which had been caused by a want of proper food, and constant exposure. None can fully realize the intense agony, the horrid suspense and wretchedness felt by these unfortunate men, but those who have had a like experience. Indeed, their sufferings were beyond description. Only a few could receive medical treatment, and that scarcely worth mentioning, while in every part of camp were as brave and loyal soldiers as any that had ever taken up arms in defence of freedom, suffering and dying in a manner that might have shocked even the rude sensibilities of an American savage. It seemed that the more bitter our anguish became, the more delighted were our fiendish keepers. Not satisfied with the cruelties inflicted upon us, they even carried their animosities beyond this life, and declined to give a Christian burial to our dead. I will not now longer dwell upon this subject. It is too painful to contemplate.

July 13th, one of the men in attempting to procure some clean water to drink, passed a little beyond the dead line, and was fired upon by two of the guards almost simultaneously. Both balls missed him, but took effect upon two other men, killing one of them immediately.

July 27th, another of our men was shot. He received a horrible wound in the head, and was carried out of camp in a dying condition.

August 4th, still another was shot, receiving a severe wound through the body. August 6th, another cold-blooded murder was committed.

One of the men, passing a little too near the stockade, was shot dead by a guard on duty. It had become dangerous to pass at the regular crossing. The sentinels seemed to be more vigilant than ever before in watching for opportunities to shoot down our poor unarmed men. No one was safe. No warning was given to a thoughtless intruder. The first thing one would know of his terrible condition after passing the fatal line, was a quick, sharp report, a groan, and all was over — another murder was committed. About the middle of August, the rate of mortality was about eighty per day. Diarrhœa and scurvy were the chief scourges of the camp. The fearful work of death was visible every where around us. I have frequently seen as many as thirty dead men lying in a row at the prison gate to be carried out for burial. It was sad, indescribably so, to see these brave men dying so far from home and its hallowed associations. No fond parents near to speak words of comfort and tenderness. None able to minister to their temporal necessities — none who could alleviate their sufferings. Alone they must writhe in the agonies of death — alone to die.

It was under such circumstances of darkness and misery, that the shining truths of Christianity shone out before men in their unsurpassed glory and heavenly beauty. Many a freed, joyous spirit, went from that foul, loathsome prison, to immortal life and happiness.

Thus far, only some of the physical sufferings consequent to our imprisonment have been briefly mentioned; it is now time to refer, for a few moments, to the intense mental trials and afflictions which we prisoners experienced.

In my diary, under date of August 24th, I find the following: "I believe the loss of health, exposure to privations, and physical suffering consequent upon the manner of life in which we are now compelled to live, are not the saddest effects of our present captivity. But that which is the most lamentable is the mental debility, which, under the present state of things, we must necessarily experience." Again, "The finer feelings — that which makes more lovely — as social being, love, affection, friendship, kindness, and courtesy, are being constantly deadened — rooted out from the heart, leaving it in a most woeful condition." Scarcely an hour in which anxiety about distant friends, suspense in regard to the future, and frequent despair, were not felt. It seems to me that the mind must have been in a state of trouble and anxiety nearly all of the time its frail tenement was suffering from confinement and disease. It was almost impossible to procure reading matter. Some of the soldiers had Bibles and Testaments, which were eagerly sought after, and read by many of the men.

It was with great difficulty one could think very attentively about other subjects than home and release from imprisonment. A topic for conversation might be introduced among a squad of men; perhaps they might talk about it for a few moments, but it would soon be dropped, and home, friends, and possibility or probability of exchange would come up for discussion. Men—brave men, indeed—became gloomy and despondent. Light faded from the once brilliant, fiery eye; the color disappeared from the manly countenance; manhood seemed to forget itself; the entire man was speedily drifting toward a fearful ruin. Hope had nearly vanished. The mind was laboring under intense agony. To some the burden was too much, and they have never recovered from its baneful effects. Others have nearly recovered, but the scars remain.

September 7th, the removal of the prisoners from Camp Sumter to other portions of the Confederacy was commenced. We were induced by the rebel authorities to believe that this unexpected movement was for a general exchange. With this belief our men could be sent away with only a small force guarding them, which was a consideration of no little importance with the rebels just at that time.

Suddenly stricken down with a violent attack of the scurvy, I was unable to leave with my detachment, and was left with the sick in camp. After suffering several days, I managed to get out with the first squad of sick which left for Florence, South Carolina. I was quite weak and feeble when I arrived at Florence, but a change of climate and diet rapidly improved my condition, and in a few days I was able to walk about without crutches. Soon afterward I was detailed as hospital steward, and paroled.

From that time till my release, Nov. 30th, my treatment was much better than it had been while I was at Camp Sumter. But in regard to that received by the thousands of poor fellows in the prison, there was but little apparent change. They suffered from cold and hunger perhaps more than while at Andersonville.

I will here close my accounts of the sufferings of our friends. So far as I am concerned personally, I can forgive our bitter foes the cruelties which they have inflicted upon me. I do not desire revenge. That is farthest from my heart. God will punish them for their evil deeds.

They have already suffered terribly. I feel that all should now try to do whatever they can to narrow the breach which exists between them and ourselves. I have always been glad our government so nobly declined to resort to retaliation. We cannot afford to be cruel. It is our highest honor to reward good for evil.

The magnanimity of our people is beyond question, and our enemies must acknowledge it. Our arms have conquered their proud hosts; our kindness must now subdue the enmity of their hearts. We must be neither too lenient nor too severe. To the leaders who precipitated us into four years of bloodshed and war, the severest punishment which the law can give; but to the poor misguided masses, that clemency which only a noble people are capable of exercising.

RATIONS ISSUED BY THE UNITED STATES GOVERNMENT TO REBEL PRISONERS OF WAR. (Note the difference.)

Iard bread,............ 14 oz. per one ration, or 18 oz. soft bread, one ration.
Corn meal,............. 18 oz. per one ration.
Beef, ... 14 oz. per one ration.
Bacon or pork, ... 10 " " "
Beans,................... 6 qts. per 100 men.
Hominy or rice, ... 8 lbs. " "
Sugar,................... 44 " " "
R. Coffee,.............. 5 " ground, or 7 lbs. raw, per 100 men.
Tea, ... 18 oz. per 100 men.
Soap,.................... 4 " " "
Adamantine candles, 5 candles per 100 men.
Tallow candles,........ 6 " " "
Salt, ... 2 qts. " "
Molasses, ... 1 qt. " "
Potatoes, ... 30 lbs. " "

STATEMENT OF CLOTHING ISSUED TO PRISONERS OF WAR, AT FORT DELAWARE.

From Sept. 1st, 1863, to May 1st, 1864.

7,175 Pairs drawers (Canton flannel).
6,260 Shirts (flannel).
8,807 Pairs woolen stockings.
1,094 Jackets and coats.
3,480 Pairs bootees.
1,310 Pairs trowsers.
4,378 Woolen blankets.
2,680 Great coats.

Average number of prisoners, 4,489.

The following poetical description of prison life in the south is from the genial pen of an Andersonville prisoner, whose name I have not been able to learn.

UNION PRISONERS, FROM DIXIE'S SUNNY LAND.

Air — "Twenty Years Ago."

I.

Dear friends and fellow soldiers brave, come listen to our song,
About the rebel prisons, and our sojourn there so long;
Yet our wretched state and hardships great no one can understand,
But those who have endured this fate in Dixie's sunny land.

II.

When captured by the chivalry, they strip't us to the skin,
But failed to give us back again the value of a pin —
Except some lousy rags of gray, discarded by their band —
And thus commenced our prison life in Dixie's sunny land.

III.

With a host of guards surrounding us, each with a loaded gun,
We were stationed in an open plain, exposed to rain and sun;
No tent or tree to shelter us, we lay upon the sand —
Thus side by side great numbers died in Dixie's sunny land.

IV.

This was the daily "bill of fare" in that secesh saloon —
No sugar, tea or coffee there, at morning, night or noon;
But a pint of meal, ground cob and all, was served to every man,
And for want of fire we ate it raw in Dixie's sunny land.

V.

We were by these poor rations soon reduced to skin and bone,
A lingering starvation — worse than death! you can but own,
There hundreds lay, both night and day, by far too weak to stand,
Till death relieved their sufferings in Dixie's sunny land.

VI.

We poor survivors oft were tried by many a threat and bribe,
To desert our glorious Union cause, and join the rebel tribe.
Though fain were we to leave the place, we let them understand,
We had rather die than thus disgrace our flag! in Dixie's land.

VII.

Thus dreary days and nights roll'd by — yes, weeks and months untold,
Until that happy time arrived when we were all paroled.
We landed at Anapolis, a wretched looking band,
But glad to be alive and free from Dixie's sunny land.

VIII.

How like a dream those days now seem in retrospective view,
As we regain our wasted strength, all dressed in "Union Blue."
The debt we owe our bitter foe shall not have long to stand;
We shall pay it with a vengeance soon in Dixie's sunny land.

APPENDIX.

The following appendix is not as perfect as I could wish; it being very difficult to avoid errors in lists of this kind. The principal portion of the names were taken from the rebel adjutant's book at Libby Prison, during the winter and spring of 1864, by Capt. Fisher, to whom I have alluded in my preface. The remainder were compiled during my imprisonment at Columbia.

OFFICERS

OF THE

UNITED STATES ARMY AND NAVY

Prisoners of War, Libby Prison, Richmond, Va.

BRIGADIER GENERALS.

Neal Dow, 1st Brigade, 2d Division, 19 A. C.
E. P. Scammon, 3d Dept. W. V.

COLONELS.

F. A. Bartleson, 100 Ill.
C. H. Carlton, 89 O.
P. D. Cesnola, 4 N. Y. C.
Wm. G. Ely, 18 Conn.
W. P. Kindrick, 3 W. T. C.
O. A. Lawson, 3 O.
H. Le Favour, 22 Mich.
R. W. McClain, 51 O.
W. H. Powell, 2 Va. C.
Tho. E. Rose, 77 Pa.
A. D. Streight, 51 Ind.
Chas. W. Tilden, 16 Me.
A. H. Tippin, 68 Pa.
W. T. Wilson, 123 O.

LIEUT. COLONELS.

S. M. Archer, 17 Ia.
I. F. Boyd, 20 A. C.
T. F. Cavada, 114 Pa.
C. Farnsworth, 1 Conn. C.
W. A. Glenn, 89 O.
H. B. Hunter, 123 O.
A. P. Henry, 15 Ky. C.
E. L. Hays, 100 O.
H. C. Hobert, 21 Wis.
O. C. Johnson, 15 Wis.
G. C. Joslin, 15 Mass.
W. P. Lasselle, 9 Md.
W. E. McMackin, 21 Ill.
D. A. McHolland, 51 Ind.
C. H. Mortin, 84 Ill.
J. D. Mayhew, 8 Ky.
D. Miles, 79 Pa.
W. B. McCreary, 21 Mich.
R. S. Northcott, 12 Va.
M. Nichols, 18 Conn.
Wm. Price, 139 Va. M.
P. S. Piver, 77 Penn.

332 APPENDIX.

I. J. Polsley, 8 Va. V. I.
A. F. Rogers, 80 Ill.
J. P. Spofford, 79 N. Y.
J. M. Sanderson, S. O.
G. Von Helmrich, 4 Mo. C.

A. Van Schrader, A. I. G.
I. H. Wing, 3 O.
J. N. Walker, 73 Ind.
J. Williams, 25 O.
T. S. West, 24 Wis.

MAJORS.

E. N. Bates, 80 Ill.
W. T. Beatly, 2 O.
C. H. Beers, 16 Ill. C.
J. P. Collins, 29 Ind.
M. E. Clarke, 5 Mich.
D. A. Carpenter, 2 Tenn.
J. J. Edwards, 32 Mass.
G. W. Fitzsimmons, 30 Ind.
N. Goff, Jr., 4 W. Va. C.
J. H. Hooper, 15 Mass.
J. Hall, 1 Va. C.
Jno. Henry, 5 O. C.
J. B. Hill, 17 Mass.
I. H. Johnson, 11 Tenn.
S. Kovax, 54 N. Y.
W. D. Morton, 14 N. Y. C.
S. McIrvin, 2 N. Y. C.
B. B. McDonald, 101 O.

A. McMahan, 21 O.
D. M. Kercher, 10 Wis.
M. Moore, 29 Ind.
W. S. Marshall, 5 Ia.
S. Marsh, 5 Md.
J. R. Muhlman, A. A. G.
W. P. Nieper, 57 Pa.
W. N. Ovens, 1 Ky. C.
E. M. Pope, 8 N. Y. C.
L. N. Phelps, 5 Va.
A. Phillips, 77 Pa.
T. B. Rodgers, 140 Pa.
W. I. Russell, A. A. G.
I. C. Vananda, 3 O.
A. Von Mitzel, 74 Pa.
H. A. White, 13 Pa. C.
J. B. Wade, 73 Ind.
Harry White, 67 Pa.

CAPTAINS.

W. F. Armstrong, 74 O.
S. C. Arthurs, 67 Pa.
W. Airey, 15 Pa. C.
E. C. Alexander, 1 Del.
W. B. Avery, 132 N. Y.
I. A. Arthur, 8 Ky. C.
H. H. Alban, 21 O.
W. R. Adams, 89 O.
C. A. Adams, 1 Verm.
Jno. Albright, 87 Pa.
E. W. Atwood, 16 Me.
M. Boyd, 73 Ind.
Chas. Byron, 3 O.
E. Baas, 20 Ill.
L. T. Borgers, 67 Pa.
H. P. Barker, 1 R. I. C.
W. K. Boltz, 181 Pa.

H. R. Bending, 61 O.
M. R. Baldwin, 2 Wis.
C. D. Brown, 18 Conn.
W. P. Bender, 123 O.
John Bird, 14 Pa. C.
L. B. Blinn, 100 O.
D. E. Bohannon, 3 T. C.
Dav. I. Bailey, 99 N. Y.
A. J. Bigelow, 79 Ill.
Jno. Birch, 42 Ind.
D. M. Barritt, 89 O.
W. M. Beeman, 1 Va. C.
F. Barton, 10 Mass.
J. H. Barton, 1 Ky. C.
E. B. Bascom, 5 Ia.
B. V. Banks, 13 Ky.
Jno. G. Bush, 16 Ill. C.

APPENDIX. 333

W. J. Barnes, 83 N. Y.
A. Carley, 73 Ind.
H. Casker, 1 N. Y. C.
W. F. Conrad, 25 Ia.
J. W. Chamberlain, 123 O.
D. S. Caldwell, 123 O.
J. Carroll, 5 Md.
J. C. Carpenter, 67 Pa.
B. G. Casler, 154 N. Y.
C. C. Comee, 94 N. Y.
E. Charleer, 157 N. Y.
Jno. Cutler, 34 O.
R. T. Cornwall, 67 Pa.
Jno. Craig, 1 Va. Cav.
Jno. Christopher, 16 U. S.
J. P. Cummins, 9 Md.
M. A. Cochran, 16 U. S.
T. Clarke, 79 Ill.
J. Cusac, 21 O.
W. A. Collins, 10 Wis.
B. F. Campbell, 36 Ill.
S. S. Canfield, 21 O.
T. Cummins, 19 U. S.
Miles Caton, 21 O.
D. S. Cannover, 125 Ill.
G. A. Crocker, 6 N. Y. C.
W. N. Cochran, 42 Ill.
M. Callahan, 9 Md.
W. E. Conway, 9 Md.
J. P, Cummins, 9 Md.
M. C. Carns, 3 Tenn.
J. R. Copeland, 7 O. C.
A. R. Calhoun, 1 Ky.
R. S. Curd, 11 Ky. C.
E. M. Driscoll, 3 O.
W. N Deung, 51 Ind.
B. Domschke, 26 Wis.
F. B. Doten, 14 Conn.
F. W. Dillion, 1 Ky. C.
H. C. Davis, 18 Conn.
Jno. Dunce, A. D. C.
W. H. Douglas, C. S.
K. S. Dygert, 16 Mich.
H. Dietz, 45 N. Y.
J. M. Dushane, 142 N. Y.

G. C. Davis, 4 Me
R. H. Day, 56 Pa.
E. Day, Jr., 89 O.
R. Dinsmore, 5 Pa.
E. J. Dunn, 1 Tenn. C.
E. Dillingham, 10 Va.
F. C. Dirks, 1 Tenn.
H. H. Eberhardt, 120 O.
B. F. Evers, 100 O.
S. H. Ewing, 26 O.
M. Ewen, 21 Wis.
A. Eglin, 45 O.
Jno. M. Flinn, 51 Ind.
E. A. Fobes, C. S.
B. F. Fischer, S. O.
A. Field, 94 N. Y.
J. B. Fay, 154 N. Y.
E. Frey, 82 Ill.
W. Forrester, 24 O.
J. W. Foster, 42 Ill.
Di Getman, 10 N. Y. C.
G. C. Gordon, 24 Mich.
G. W. Green, 19 Ind.
H. W. Gimber, 150 Pa.
W. L. Gray, 151 Pa.
J. H. Green, 100 O.
Chas. Gustaveson, 15 Wis.
J. F. Gallaher, 2 O.
J. Goetz, 22 Mich.
A. G. Galbraith, 22 Mich.
J. Gates, 33 O.
O. C. Gatch, 89 O.
S. A. Glenn, 89 O.
J. W. Grose, 18 Ky.
B. Grafton, 64 O.
H. H. Gregg, 18 Pa. C.
Jas. Galt, A. Q. M.
M. Gallagher, 2 N. Y. C.
Dan'l Hay, 80 Ill.
A. Hodge, 80 Ill.
J. G. Hagler, 5 Tenn.
A. M. Heyer, 10 Va. C.
J. Hendricks, 1 N. Y. C.
John Heil, 45 N. Y.
A. Haack, 18 N. Y.

S. G. Hamlin, 134 N. Y.
W. L. Hubbell, 17 Conn.
P. H. Hart, 19 Ind.
A. Heffley, 142 Pa.
W. W. Hant, 100 O.
Chas. Hasty, 2 N. Y. C.
A. G. Hamilton, 12 Ky.
T. Handy, 79 Ill.
V. K. Hart, 19 U. S.
H. Hescock, 1 Mo. A.
R. Harkness, 10 Wis.
H. E. Hawkins, 78 Ill.
C. C. Huntley, 16 Ill.
J. B. Herold, 9 Md.
S. C. Honeycutt, 2 E. T.
S. Irvin, 3 Iowa.
S. F. Jones, 80 Ill.
J. M. Imbrie, 3 O.
R. Johnson, 6 N. Y. C.
F. Irich, 45 N. Y.
J. C. Johnson, 149 Pa.
F. R. Josselyn, 11 Mass.
R. O. Ivro, 10 Mass.
D. I. Jones, 1 Ky. C.
J. S. Jackson, 22 Ill.
J. M. Johnson, 6 Ky.
J. A. Johnson, 11 Ky. C.
J. T. Jennings, 45 O.
W. M. Kendall, 73 Ind.
E. M. Kech, 5 Md.
S. B. King, 12 Pa. C.
A. M. Keeler, 22 Mich.
D. A. Kelly, 1 Ky. C.
J. Kelly, 73 Pa.
D. F. Kelly, 73 Pa.
J. Kennedy, 73 Pa.
W. D. Lucas, 5 N. Y. C.
R. F. Lownsberry, 10 N. Y. C.
L. P. Lovett, 5 Ky.
John Lucas, 5 Ky.
J. W. Lewis, 4 Ky. C.
E. M. Lee, 5 Mich. C.
J. E. Love, 8 Ks.
J. R. Land, 66 Ind.
S. McKee, 14 Ky. C.

D. H. Mull, 73 Ind.
D. A. McHolland, 51 Ind.
J. B. McRoberts, 3 O.
McMoore, 29 Ind.
W. M. Morris, 93 Ill.
H. C. McGuiddy, 1 T. C.
F. Mennert, 5 Md.
E. J. Matthewson, 18 Conn.
W. F. Martins, 14 Mass. A.
P. Marsh, 67 Pa.
D. B. Meany, 13 Pa. C.
C. C. Moses, 58 Pa.
C. A. Mann, 5 Ill. C.
S. Marsh, 5 Md.
J. McMahon, 94 N. Y.
E. A. Mass, 88 Pa.
A. J. Makepeace, 19 Ind.
H. H. Mason, 2 N. Y. C.
C. W. Medcalf, 42 Ind.
J. S. McDowell, 77 Pa.
J. G. Williams, 51 Ill.
J. Meagher, 40 O.
W. McGinnis, 74 Ill.
J. M. McComas, 9 Md.
A. W. Metcalf, 14 N. Y. C.
M. R. Milsaps, 2 E. T.
A. Marney, 2 E. T.
W. M. Murray, 2 E. T.
J. C. Martin, 1 Tenn. A.
S. Meade, 11 N. Y.
W. A. Noel, 5 Md.
H. Noble, 9 Md.
T. W. Olcott, 134 N. Y.
E. O'Brien, 29 Mo.
N. C. Pace, 80 Ill.
J. D. Phelps, 78 Ind.
F. A. Patterson, 3 Va. C.
J. F. Porter, 14 N. Y. C.
J. A. Pennfield, 5 N. Y. C.
E. Porter, 154 N. Y.
S. V. Pool, 154 N. Y.
F. Place, 157 N. Y.
S. H. Pillsbury, 5 Me.
R. Pollock, 14 Pa. C.
G. S. Pierce, 19 U. S.

APPENDIX.

F. W. Perry, 10 Wis.
E. J. Pennypacker, 18 Pa. C.
W. F. Pickerill, 5 Ia.
J. E. Page, 5 Ia.
J. A. Richley, 73 Ind.
M. Russell, 51 Ind.
P. C. Reed, 3 O.
W. C. Rossman, 3 O.
J. F. Randolph, 123 O.
A. Robbins, 123 O.
C. H. Riggs, 123 O.
O. H. Rosenbaum, 123 O.
W. Rowan, Indp. C.
M. Rollins, 2 Wis.
J. C. Rose, 4 Mo. C.
Thos. Reed, 1 Va.
W. A. Robinson, 77 Ia.
B. F. Riggs, 18 Ky.
N. S. Randall, 2 O.
J. A. Rice, 73 Ill.
W. J. Robb, 1 Va.
A. Rodgers, 4 Ky. C.
C. Rowan, 96 Ill.
S. B. Ryder, 5 N. Y. C.
C. Reynolds, 8 Tenn.
W. H. Robins, 2 E. Tenn.
J. A. Russell, 93 Ill.
W. W. Searce, 51 Ind.
W. A. Swayze, 3 O.
D. D. Smith, 1 Tenn. C.
E. Szabad, A. D. C.
H. W. Sawyer, 1 N. J. C.
E. A. Shepherd, 110 O.
D. Schirtz, 12 Pa. C.
Geo. L. Schell, 88 Pa.
S. A. Urquhard, C. S.
G. H. Starr, 88 Pa.
J. R. Stone, 157 N. Y.
Wm. Syring, 45 N. Y.
R. Scofield, 1 Va. C.
T. M. Shoemaker, 100 O.
J. A. Scammerhorn, 112 Ind.
J. C. Shroad, 77 Pa.

A. H. Stanton, 16 U. S.
R. H. Spencer, 10 Wis.
S. A. Spencer, 82 O.
E. L. Smith, 19 U. S.
J. P. Singer, 33 O.
A. P. Seuter, 2 E. Tenn.
P. S. Scott, 85 Ill.
T. Thornton, 161 N. Y.
John Teed, 116 Pa.
O. Templeton, 107 Pa.
H. D. Taylor, 100 O.
B. E. Thomson, A. D. C.
T. Ten Eyck, 18 U. S.
A. Tubbs, 9 Ky. C.
T. Thornton, 5 U. S.
G. C. Urwiler, 67 Pa.
J. D. Underdown, 2 E. D.
J. W. Vanderhoef, 45 N. Y.
G. M. Van Buren, 6 N. Y. C
A. Wilson, 80 Ill.
W. R. Wright, 80 Ill.
J. A. Wistlake, 73 Ind.
Wm. Walleck, 51 Ind.
G. W. Warner, 18 Conn.
C. W. White, 3 Va. C.
W. Willets, 7 Mich.
J. C. Whiteside, 94 N. Y.
T. E. Wentworth, 16 Me.
W. C. Wilson, 104 N. Y.
H. C. White, 94 N. Y.
C. C. Widdis, 150 Pa.
Geo. M. White, 1 Va.
W. H. Williams, 4 N. Y. C.
P. Wellsheimer, 21 Ill.
H. P. Wands, 22 Mich.
W. B. Wicker, 21 O.
J. E. Wilkens, 112 Ill.
J. G. Wild, 9 N. Y. C.
J. H. Whelan, A. Q. M.
E. A. Wolcott, 16 Ill.
M. G. Whitney, 29 Mo.
H. Zeis, 80 Ill.
J. C. Slover, 3 E. T.

APPENDIX.

LIEUTENANTS.

M. Ahern, 10 Va.
C. L. Alstaed, 54 N. Y.
S. A. Albro, 80 Ill.
Jas. Adams, 80 Ill.
W. A. Adair, 51 Ind.
H. Appel, 1 Md. C.
R. W. Anderson, 122 O.
H. F. Anshutz, 12 Va.
F. S. Armstrong, 122 O.
H. M. Anderson, 3 Me.
J. H. Ahlert, 45 N. Y.
C. L. Anderson, 3 Ia.
G. D. Acker, 123 O.
H. W. Adams, 37 Ill.
E. E. Andrews, 22 Mich.
A. Allee, 16 Ill. C.
H. S. Albin, 79 Ill.
R. J. Allen, 2 E. Tenn.
P. Atkin, 2 E. Tenn.
A. B. Alger, 22 O. B.
J. W. Austin, 5 Ia.
Mich. Ahern, 10 Va.
H. C. Abernathy, 16 Ill. C.
T. I. Brownell, 51 Ind.
J. W. Barlow, 51 Ind.
J. G. Blue, 3 O.
O. P. Barnes, 3 O.
G. W. Bailey, 3 O.
J. L. Brown, 73 Ind.
A. H. Booher, 73 Ind.
J. F. Bedwell, 80 O.
W. Blancherd, 2 U. S. C.
B. F. Blair, 123 O.
H. S. Bevington, 123 O.
F. W. Boyd, 123 O.
F. A. Breckenridge, 123 O.
Jno. D. Babb, 5 Md.
J. G. W. Brueting, 5 Md.
T. J. Borchers, 67 Pa.
W. Bierbower, 87 Pa.
G. C. Bleak, 8 Me.
W. H. Berry, 5 Ill. C.
H. Bath, 45 N. Y.

L. C. Bisby, 16 Me.
M. Beedle, 123 N. Y.
C. T. Barclay, 149 Pa.
J. D. Bisby, 16 Me.
S. G. Boone, 88 Pa.
D. S. Bartram, 17 Conn.
Jas. Burns, 57 Pa.
S. H. Ballard, 6 Mich. C.
S. T. Boughton, 71 Pa.
M. M. Bassett, 53 Ill.
R. Y. Bradford, 2 W. T.
W. Bricker, 3 Pa. C.
J. T. Brush, 100 O.
O. G. Ballow, 100 O.
J. F. Baird, 1 Va.
E. G. Birun, 3 Mass.
G. E. Blaire, 17 O.
Jas. Biggs, 123 Ill.
Y. Bickham, 19 U. S.
J. P. Brown, 15 U. S.
M. C. Bryant, 42 Ill.
O. B. Brandt, 17 O.
G. W. Button, 22 Mich.
C. A. Burdick, 10 Wis.
J. L. Brown, 73 Ind.
F. T. Bennett, 18 U. S.
Jno. Baird, 89 O.
W. O. Butler, 10 Wis.
D. A. Bannister, 59 O.
Jno. Bradford, C. S.
G. R. Barse, 5 Mich. C.
C. P. Butler, 29 Ind.
E. P. Brooks, 6 Wis.
W. L. Brown, R. O.
G. W. Buffum, 1 Wis.
Guy Bryan, 18 Pa. C.
S. S. Baker, 6 Mo.
H. Bader, 29 Mo.
S. H. Byers, 5 Ia.
W. L. Bath, 132, N. Y.
Geo. M. Bush, U. S. T.
A. H. Bassett, 79 Ill.
J. C. Colwell, 16 Ill. C.

APPENDIX. 337

Jno. H. Conn, 1 Va. C.
S. Carpenter, 3 O.
W. A. Curry, 3 O.
R. J. Connelly, 73 Ind.
A. M'Callahan, 73 Ind.
J. W. Custed, 23 Ind.
J. D. Cook, 6 Ia.
J. Carothers, 78 O.
S. R. Colloday, 6 Pa. C.
T. B. Calver, 123 O.
L. B. Comins, 17 Mass.
J. H. Cook, 5 Md.
J. H. Chandler, 5 Md.
E. D. Carpenter, 18 Conn.
H. F. Cowles, 18 Conn.
W. Cristopher, 2 Va. C.
J. Q. Carpenter, 150 Pa.
H. B. Chamberlain, 97 N. Y.
T. J, Crossley, 57 Pa.
J. A. Carman, 107 Pa.
J. A. Coffin, 157 N. Y.
D. J. Conelly, 63 N. Y.
J. U. Childs, 16 Me.
D. B. Caldwell, 75 O.
W. B. Cook, 140 Pa.
J. W. Chandler, 1 Va. C.
H. A. Curtice, 157 N. Y.
J. Chatborn, 150 Pa.
S. E. Cary, 13 Mass.
A. Cloadt, 119 N. Y.
J. Clement, 15 Ky. C.
G. A. Chandler, 15 Mo.
J. H. Cain, 104 N. Y.
B. Coles, 2 N. Y. C.
J. B. Carlisle, 2 Va.
G. B. Coleman, 1 Mass. C.
G. A. Coffin, 29 Ind.
J. L. Cox, 21 Ill.
W. N. Culbertson, 30 Ind.
F. G. Cochran, 77 Pa.
Geo. Cleghorn, 21 O.
W. W. Calkins, 104 Ill.
G. Celly, 4 O. C.
H. B. Crawford, 2 Ill.
T. S. Coleman, 12 Ky. C.

O. L. Cole, 51 Ill.
Rudolph Curtis, 4 Ky. C.
M. C. Causton, 19 U. S.
E. Cottingham, 35 O.
W. Clifford, 16 U. S.
M. Cohen, 4 Ky. C.
A. S. Cooper, 9 Md.
J. F. Carter, 9 Md.
W. H. Crawford, 2 E. T.
C. W. Catlett, 2 E. T.
C. J. Carlin, 151 N. Y.
H. Cuniffe, 13 Ill.
C. H. Coasdorph, 8 V. C.
G. W. Carey, 65 Ind.
J. G. Doughty, 51 Ind.
J. A Dilan, 51 Ind.
A. F. Dooley, 51 Ind.
T. B. Dewies, 2 U. S.
M. Diemer, 10 Mo.
V. R. Davis, 123 O.
C. G. Davis, 1 Mass. C.
L. N. Dueherney, 1 Mass. C.
J. R. Day, 3 Me.
J. S. Devine, 71 Pa.
Geo. A. Deering, 16 Me.
A. Dixon, 104 N. Y.
Jno. Daily, 104 N. Y.
C. H. Drake, 142 Pa.
B. Davis, 71 Pa.
A. K. Dunkel, 114 Pa.
F. Donyley, 27 R. I.
J. W. Drake, 136 N. Y.
C. D. Dillard, 7 Ia.
J. W. Day, 17 Mass.
J. M. Dushane, 142 Pa.
O. G. Deugton, 100 O.
T. G. Darnin, 16 U. S.
H. C. Dunn, 10 Ky.
W. G. Dutton, 67 Pa.
L. Drake, 22 Mich.
E. J. Davis, 44 Ill.
M. V. Dickey, 94 O.
Jno. Dugan, 35 Ind.
Thos. J. Dean, 5 Mich.
Jno. Davidson, 6 N. Y. A.

APPENDIX.

W. A. Daily, 8 Pa. C.
E. H. Duncan, 2 E. T.
A. Dieffenbach, 73 Pa.
C. L. Edmunds, 67 Pa.
D. C. Edwards, 2 Md.
J. Egan, 69 Pa.
S. Edmiston, 89 O.
W. H. Ellenwood, 10 Wis.
C. W. Earle, 96 Ill.
G. H. Erickson, 57 N. Y.
Geo. W. Fish, 3 O.
A. Frey, 73 Ind.
J. A. Francis, 18 Conn.
W. Flick, 67 Pa.
J. M. Fales, 1 R. I. C.
L. P. Fortescue, 29 Pa.
M. Fellows, 149 Pa.
W. Fenner, 2 R. I. C.
G. D. Forsyth, 100 O.
G. H. Fowler, 100 O.
J. C. Fisler, 7 Ind. B.
T. C. Freman, 18 U. S.
R. J. Fisher, 17 Mo.
Chas. Fritze, 24 Ill.
J. A. Flemming, 90 N. Y.
E. F. Foster, 30 Ind.
H. Fairchild, 10 Wis.
O. P. Fairchild, 89 O.
W. H. Follette, Mass. A.
A. W. Fritchie, 26 Mo.
I. Fontaine, 73 Pa.
E. H. Fobes, 131 N. Y.
D. D. Fox, 16 Ill. C.
A. Gude, 51 Ind.
H. Gamble, 73 Ind.
Jno. A. Garces, 1 Md. C.
Th. G. Good, 1 Md. C.
C. M Gross, 100 O.
S. L. Gilman, 3 M.
G. W. Grant, 88 Pa.
A. Goodwin, 82 O.
O. Grierson, 45 N.Y.
F. C. Gay, 11 Pa.
C. F. Gutland, 134 N. Y.
E. G. Gorgus, 90 Pa.

J. Gilmore, 79 N. Y.
S. P. Gamble, 63 Pa.
G. L. Garrett, 4 Mo. C.
F. M. Gilleland, 15 Ky.
Geo. H. Gamble, 8 Ill. C.
D. Garlet, 77 Pa.
T. Gross, 21 Ill.
H. Gerhardt, 24 Ill.
R. II. Gray, 15 U. S.
J. M. Goff, 10 Wis.
W. G. Galloway, 15 U. S.
J. H. Gageby, 19 U. S.
R. C. Gates, 18 U. S.
C. W. Green, 44 Ind.
J. B. Gore, 15 Ill.
J. A. Green, 13 Pa. C.
W. W. Glazier, 2 N. Y. C.
E. Gordon, 81 Ind.
A. L. Gates, 10 Wis.
M. Gray, 13 N. Y.
W. G. Griffin, 112 Ill.
C. Greble, 8 Mich. C.
Geo. Good, 84 Pa.
M. E. Green, 5 Md. C.
J. B. Holmes, 6 O.
Jno. Hood, 80 Ill.
R. J. Harmer, 80 Ill.
W. H. Harvey, 51 Ind.
G. D. Hand, 51 Ind.
D. H. Harns, 3 O.
Jno. Haideman, 129 Ill.
H. S. Horton, 101 Pa.
W. E. Hodge, 5 Md.
W. Hawkins, 5 Md.
D. W. Hakes, 18 Conn.
J. D. Higgins, 18 Conn.
W. Heffner, 67 Pa.
F. A. Hubble, 67 Pa.
J. C. Hagenbach, 67 Pa.
J. Hersh, 87 Pa.
J. Hall, 87 Pa.
P. Horney, 110 O.
T. J. Higginson, M. C.
J. G. Hallenberg, 1 O.
A. Hauf, 54 N. Y.

APPENDIX. 339

H. H. Hinds, 57 Pa.
Thos. Huggins, 2 N. Y.
Eug. Hepp, 82 Ill.
C. P. Heffley, 142 Pa.
J. M. Henry, 154 N. Y.
G. Halpin, 116 Pa.
E. H. Harkness, 6 Pa. C.
J. D. Hatfield, 53 Ill.
A. W. Hayes, 34 O.
J. F. Hammond, R. B.
H. Hubbard, 12 N. Y.
W. S. Hatcher, 30 O.
Jno. Hine, 100 O.
M. B. Helmes, 1 Va. C.
C. B. Hall, 1 Va. C.
Eli Holden, 1 Va. C.
B. Howe, 21 Ill.
P. W. Houlchen, 16 U. S.
C. D. Henry, 4 O. C.
J. Hanon, 115 Ill.
C. E. Harrison, 89 O.
Geo. Harris, 79 Ind.
W. B. Hamilton, 22 Mich.
S. S. Holbruck, 15 U. S.
L. D. Henkley, 10 Wis.
E. G. Higby, 33 O.
W. M. Hudson, 92 O.
H. Horway, 78 Ill.
C. F. Hall, 13 Mich.
G. C. Houston, 2 N. Y. C.
P. A. Hagen, 7 Md.
J. R. Hutchinson, 2 Va. C.
G. W. Hale, 101 O.
R. Huey, 2 E. T.
W. P. Hodge, 2 E. T.
E. Harbour, 2 E. T.
B. F. Herrington, 18 Pa. C.
Jas. Heslit, 3 Pa. C.
Jno. Hoffman, 5 Ia.
T. W. Hayes, 5 Ia.
M. Hoffman, 5 Ia.
J. M. Holloway, 6 Ind.
C. M. Hart, 45 Pa.
J. P. Jones, 55 O.
C. L. Irwin, 78 Ill.

C. W. Jones, 16 Pa. C.
P. O. Jones, adj't, 2 N. Y. C.
J. A. Jones, 21 Ill.
J. H. Jenkins, 21 Wis.
R. W. Jackson, 21 Wis.
T. W. Johnson, 10 N. Y. C.
H. P. Jordan, 9 Md.
H. Jones, 5 U. S. C.
R. B. Jones, 2 E. T.
H. H. James, 6 Ind. C.
John King, 5 Ill. C.
M. D. King, 3 O.
A. J. Kuhn, 5 Md.
H. V. Knight, 20 Mich.
J. S. Kephart, 5 Md. C.
Jas. Kerin, 6 U. S. C.
J. B. King, 10 N. Y. C.
G. Keyes, 18 Conn.
J. N. Kibbee, 18 Conn.
A. Kresge, 67 Pa.
R. O. Knowles, 110 O.
H. Kendler, 45 N. Y.
M. Kupp, 167 Pa.
Jas. Kane, 13 Pa. C.
R. C. Knaggs, A. D. C.
J. Kunkel, 45 N. Y.
J. W. Kennedy, 134 N. Y.
J. C. Kellogg, 6 Mich.
D. O. Kelly, 100 O.
J. D. Kautz, 1 Ky. C.
T. A. Krocks, 77 Pa.
T. D. Kimball, 88 Ind.
Wm. Krueger, 2 Mo.
E. E. Knoble, 21 Ky.
E. M. Knowles, 42 Ind.
J. Keniston, 100 Ill.
S. Koach, 100 Ill.
C. E. Keath, 19 Ill.
Theo. Kendall, 15 U. S.
H. B. Kelly, 6 Ky. C.
D. F. Kittrell, 3 E. T.
W. S. Lyon, 23 O.
T. Lennig, 6 Pa. C.
F. A. Leyton, 18 Ind.
A. W. Loomis, 18 Conn.

APPENDIX.

A. H. Lindsay, 18 Conn.
L. Lapton, 116 O.
W. H. Locke, 18 Conn.
J. Leydecker, 45 N. Y.
L. Lindemeyer, 45 N. Y.
H. G. Lombard, 4 Mich.
W. L. Laws, 18 Pa. C.
A. T. Lamson, 104, N. Y.
A. W. Locklin, 94 N. Y.
G. R. Lodge, 53 Ill.
T. Lloyd, 6 Ind. C.
C. H. Livingston, 1 Va. C.
J. L. Leslie, 18 Pa. C.
D. R. Locke, 8 Ky. C.
J. Ludlow, 5 U. S. A.
A. Leonard, 71 N. Y.
W. J. Lintz, 8 Tenn.
Jno. McAdams, 10 Va.
L. Markbreit, A. D. C.
J. McKinstry, 16 Ill. C.
T. Milward, 31 O.
W. H. McDill, 80 Ill.
W. S. Marshall, 51 Ind.
J. H. Murdock, 3 O.
C. A. Maxwell, 3 O.
H. S. Murdock, 73 Ind.
J. D. Munday, 73 Ind.
J. S. Mettee, 5 Md.
Jno. McCumas, 5 Md.
W. J. Morris, 5 Md.
T. F. McGinnes, 18 Conn
F. McKeag, 18 Conn.
H. Morningstar, 87 Pa.
J. S. Manning, 100 O.
Thos. Mosbey, 12 Pa. C.
D. McNeil, 13 Pa. C.
W. A. Murry, 106 N. Y.
H. Moaltin, 1 U. S.
L. Mayer, 12 Pa. C.
W. J. McCounelee, 4 Ia.
D. McCully, 75 O.
O. Mussehl, 68 N. Y.
H. H. Moseley, 25 O.
Thos. Myers, 107 Pa.
C. Murry, 15 Mo.

B. N. Mann, 17 Mass.
J. A. Mitchell, 82 O.
A. McDade, 154 N. Y.
J. A. Mendenhall, 75 O.
J. R. Mell, 82 Ill.
V. Mylieus, 68 N. Y.
F. Moran, 73 N. Y.
J. Mooney, 107 Pa.
F. Murphy, 97 N. Y.
G. H. Morisey, 12 Ia. Q. M.
H. E. Mosher, 12 N. Y. C.
S. T. Merwin, 18 Conn.
Thos. Maver, 100 O.
T. H. McKee, 21 Ill.
J. W. Messick, 42 Ind.
D. F. McKay, 18 Pa.
R. G. McKay, 1 Mich.
Wm. McEboy, 3 Ill.
N. S. McKee, 21 Ill.
J. Mitchell, 79 Ill.
J. McGowan, 29 Ind.
M. Mahon, 16 U. S.
J. F. Mackey, 16 U. S.
C. H. Morgan, 21 Wis.
A. S. Mathews, 22 Mich.
J. S. Mahony, 15 U. S.
S. McNeal, 51 O.
L. C. Mead, 22 Mich.
A. U. McCane, 2 O.
M. V. Morrison, 32 O.
A. H. Makinson, 10 Wis.
W. H. Mead, 6 Ky. C.
A. Morse, 78 Ill.
A. Morris, 4 Ky. C.
J. McKinley, 28 O.
H. Morey, 10 N. Y. C.
G. W. Moore, 9 Md.
H. F. Meyer, 9 Md.
R. A. Moon, 6 Mich. C.
M. M. Moore, 6 Mich. C.
Jno. Millis, 66 Ind.
J. McDonald, 2 E. T.
J. McColgen, 7 O. C.
D. T. Moore, 2 E. T.
J. H. Mason, 21 O.

APPENDIX. 341.

J. McBeth, 45 O.
R. H. Montgomery, 5 U. S. C.
F. Moore, 73 Pa.
J. McGovern, 73 Pa.
A. McNiece, 73 Pa.
G. Maw, 80 O.
J. F. Morgan, 17 Mich.
C. Miller, 14 Ill. C.
W. J. Nowlan, 14 N. Y.
A. N. Norris, 107 Pa.
Wm. Nelson, 13 U. S.
J. C. Norcross, 2 Mass. C.
J. F. Newbrandt, 4 Mo. C.
Wm. Nyce, 2 N. Y. C.
B. H. Niemeger, 11 Ky. C.
O. P. Norris, 111 O.
Jno. O'Connor, 59 O.
O. C. Oug, 2 Va. C.
E. W. Pelton, 2 Md.
E. W. Parcey, 80 Ill.
S. B. Piper, 3 O.
G. A. Pottee, 2 Ky.
J. B. Pumphrey, 123 O.
W. G. Purnell, 6 Md.
C. G. A. Peterson, 1 R. I. C.
E. B. Parker, 1 R. I. C.
Henry S. Platt, 11 Mich.
E. C. Parker, 94 N. Y.
H. C. Potter, 18 Pa. C.
T. Paulding, 6 U. S. C.
J. F. Poole, 1 Va. C.
J. L. Powers, 107 N. Y.
D. B. Pettijohn, 2 U. S.
G. H. Potts, 75 O.
C. P. Potts, 151 Pa.
E. Potter, 6 Mich.
E. L. Palmer, 57 N. Y.
J. S. Paul, 122 O.
Z. R. Prather, 116 Ill.
G. Pentzel, 11 N. Y.
Jas. Perley, 13 Mich.
H. Perleen, 2 O.
J. V. Patterson, 1 O. C.
W. N. Paxton, 140 Pa.
C. Powell, 42 O.

L. D. Phelps, 8 Pa. C.
C. M. Brutzman, 7 Wis.
A. E. Patelin, 10 Wis.
M. B. Pulliam, 11 Ky. C.
R. H. Pond, 12 U. S.
Wm. P. Pierce, 11 Ky. C.
S. B. Pettrie, 126 O.
Wm. Randall, 80 Ill.
E. W. Pelton, 2 Md.
Jno. Ritchie, 3 O.
J. C. Roney, 3 O.
Wm. Reynolds, 73 Ind.
A. C. Roach, 51 Ind.
E. Reynolds, 1 Tenn. C.
E. Reed, 3 O.
J. M. Rothrock, 5 Mo.
J. P. Rockwell, 18 Conn.
J. Ruff, 67 Pa.
J. F. Robinson, 67 Pa.
W. F. Randolph, 5 U. S. A.
John Ryan, 69 Pa.
W. E. Rockwell, 134 N. Y.
J. H. Russel, 12 Mass.
J. O. Rockwell, 97 N. Y.
J. A. Richardson, 2 N. Y. C.
N. A. Robinson, 4 Me.
H. E. Rulon, 114 Pa.
H. Richardson, 19 Ind.
J. Remie, 11 Mass.
Geo. Ring, 100 O.
D. P. Rennie, 73 O.
T. J. Ray, 49 O.
W. L. Retilley, 51 O.
G. W. Robertson, 22 Mich.
J. M. Rader, 8 Tenn.
S. H. Reynolds, 42 O.
E. W. Rubbs, 1 E. T.
G. F. Robinson, 80 O.
L. S. Smith, 14 N. Y.
D. J. Shepherd, 5 Ky. C.
H. Silver, 16 Ill. C.
G. Scuttermore, 80 Ill.
Th. Segar, 80 Ill.
D. B. Stevenson, 3 O.
E. E. Sharp, 51 Ind.

APPENDIX.

J. G. Spalding, 2 U. S. C.
A. Stole, 6 U. S.
D. M. V. Stuart, 10 Mo.
M. H. Smith, 123 O.
T. H. Stewart, 5 Md.
John Sachs, 5 Md.
Jno. Sweadner, 5 Md.
J. F. Shuyler, 123 O.
C. H. Sowro, 123 O.
E. L. Schroeder, 5 Md.
G. W. Simpson, 67 Pa.
A. G. Scranton, 18 Conn.
J. Smith, 67 Pa.
C. P. Stroman, 87 Pa.
A. M. Stark, 110 O.
H. L. Sibley, 116 O.
S. Stearns, 4 Me.
G. L. Snyder, 104 N. Y.
A. W. Sprague, 24 Mich.
Geo. Schuele, 45 N. Y.
H. B. Seeley, 86 N. Y.
W. S. Stevens, 104 N. Y.
E. Schroeders, 74 Pa.
G. C. Stevens, 154 N. Y.
D. C. Sears, 96 N. Y.
H. Schroeder, 82 Ill.
J. B. Samson, 12 Mass.
Jno. Sullivan, 7 R. I.
M. R. Small, 6 Md.
E. Shepard, 6 O. C.
J. M. Steele, 1 Va.
C. Smith, 4 N. Y. C.
Jno. Sterling, 3 Ind.
F. Spencer, 17 O.
A. W. Songer, 21 Ill.
Wm. Stewart, 16 U. S.
W. H. Smith, 16 U. S.
J. D. Simpson, 10 Ind.
F. Schweinfurth, 24 Ill.
A. C. Spafford, 21 O.
E. G. Spalding, 22 Mich.
E. S. Scott, 89 O.
A. C. Shaeffer, 2 N. Y. C.
H. C. Smith, 2 Del.
Jno. Spindler, 73 Ill.

G. L. Sollers, 9 Md.
L. L. Stone, Q. M.
R. F. Scott, 11 Ky. C.
J. C. Shaw, 7 O. C.
L. W. Sutherland, 126 O.
T. B. String, 11 Ky. C.
Chas. Sutler, 39 N. Y.
Jno. H. Stevens, 5 Me.
Chas. Trommel, 3 O.
H. H. Tillotson, 73 Ind.
A. N. Thomas, 73 Ind.
D. Turner, 118 Ill.
Ira Tyler, 118 Ill.
M. Tiffany, 18 Conn.
H. O. Thayer, 67 Pa.
A. A. Taylor, 122 Pa.
R. Tyler, 6 Md.
R. Thompson, 67 Pa.
L. Thompson, 2 U. S. C.
M. Tower, 13 Mass.
E. A. Tuthill, 104 N. Y.
J. R. Titus, 3 U. S. C.
H. Temple, 2 N. Y. C.
E. M. B. Timoney, 15 U. S.
G. W. Thomas, 10 Wis.
H. C. Taylor, 21 Wis.
A. J. Tuter, 2 O.
R. F. Thorn, 5 Ky. C.
S. H. Tresoutheck, 18 Pa. C
J. Turner, Q. M.
H. Taylor, 65 Ind.
A. J. W. Ullen, 3 O.
T. R. Uptigrove, 73 Ind.
M. Undutch, 9 Md.
G. A. Vanness, 73 Ind.
Geo. Veltford, 54 N. Y.
R. N. Vannetter, 1 Mich. C.
D. Vansbury, 4 Md. B.
D. L. Wright, 51 Ind.
A. H. Wonder, 51 Ind.
Wm. Willis, 51 Ind.
I. D. Whiting, 3 O.
A. K. Wolbach, 3 O.
J. C. Woodrow, 73 Ind.
C. P. Williams, 73 Ind.

APPENDIX. 343

R. P. Wallace, 120 O.
Thos. Worthen, 118 Ill.
L. Weiser, 1 Md. C.
Wm. A Williams, 123 O.
J. W. Wooth, 5 Md.
J. B. Wilson, 5 Md.
J. E. Woodard, 18 Conn.
P. A. White, 83 Pa.
E. J. Weeks, 67 Pa.
T. J. Weakley, 110 O.
W. H. Welsh, 78 Pa.
A. Wallber, 26 Wis.
A. H. White, 27 Pa.
D. Whiston, 13 Mass.
T. Wuschow, 54 N. Y.
M. Wadsworth, 16 Me.
J. N. Whitney, 2 R. I. C.
M. F. Williams, 15 Ky.
M. Wilson, 14 Pa. C.
J. Woods, 82 Ind.

C. N. Winner, 1 O.
W. L. Watson, 21 Wis.
Wm. Willots, 22 Mich.
J. Weatherbee, 51 O.
J. M. Wasson, 40 O.
Jas. Wells, 8 Mich. C.
H. Willson, 18 Pa. C.
J. R. Weaver, 18 Pa. C.
W. H. H. Wilcox, 10 N. Y.
A. B. White, 4 Pa. C.
C. F. Weston, 21 Wis.
W. F. Wheeler, 9 Md.
N. L. Wood, Jr., 9 Md.
E. Willhort, 2 E. Tenn.
J. W. Wilshire, 45 O.
J. W. Wright, 10 Ia.
Hyde Crocker, 1 N. Y. C.
J. B. Williamson, 14 W. Va.
C. H. Yates, 96 Ill.
Sam. Leith, 132 N. Y.

NAVAL OFFICERS.

W. E. H. Fintress, A. V. Lt.
Edw. L. Hanies, Act. M.
J. F. D. Robinson, Act. M.
E. H. Sears, Ast. P. M.
Robt. M. Clark, Act. Ensg.
Simon Strunk, Act. Ensg.
E. W. Dayton, Act. Ensg.
Thos. Brown, Act. M. M.
Wm. H. Fogg, Act. M. M.
Chas. H. Stewart, Act. M. M.

Dan'l Ward, Act. M. M.
B. Johnson, 2 Act. Eng.
Jas. McCaulley, 2 Act. Eng.
Jno. B. Dick, 2 Act. Eng.
A. D. Renshaw, 3 Act. Eng.
Jno. Mee, 3 Act. Eng.
Ch. McCormick, 3 Act. Eng.
Sam. B. Ellis, 3 Act. Eng.
Henry K. Stever, 3 Act. Eng
E. J. Robinson, Pilot.

ADDITIONAL LIST OF PRISONERS.

The following is an additional list of officers captured during the spring, summer, autumn and winter of 1864, after the removal of the old prisoners from Richmond on the 7th of May. They were imprisoned at Macon, Savannah, Charleston, Columbia, Charlotte, Raleigh and Goldsborough.

COLONELS.*

J. H. Ashworth, 1 Ga. U. V.
T. H. Butler, 5 Ind. C.
S. J. Crooks, 22 N. Y. C.
J. Frasier, 140 Pa.
Pennock, Huey, 8 Pa. C.
F. C. Miller, 147 N. Y.
W. Shedd, 13 Ill.
Daniel White, 31 Me.

LIEUTENANT COLONELS.

M. P. Buffum, 4 I. R.
J. B. Conyngham, 52 Pa.
C. W. Clancy, 52 O.
M. A. Leeds, 153 O.
C. C. Matson, 6 Ind. C.
D. B. McCreary, 145 Pa.
O. Moulton, 25 Mass.
Benj. B. Morgan, 75 O.
H. R. Stoughton, 2 U. S. S. S.
A. H. Sanders, 16 Iowa.
T. J. Thorp, 1 N. Y. Drag.
G. Von Helmrick, 4 Mo. C.
G. Wallace, 47 O.

MAJORS.

J. H. Dewees, 13 Pa. C.
M. Dunn, 19 Mass.
W. N. Denny, 51 Ind.
D. English, 11 Ky. C.
C. K. Fleming, 11 Vt.
G. B. Fox, 75 O.
W. H. Forbes, 2 Mass. C.
J. H. Filer, 55 Pa.
T. J. Hasley, 11 N. Y.
W. P. Hall, 6 N. Y. C.
J. H. Isett, 8 Ind. C.
C. M. Lynch, 145 Pa.
P. McLernan, 22 N. Y. C.
C. P. Mattock, 17 Me.
P. Nelson, 66 N. Y.
J. E. Pratt, 4 Vt.
W. L. Parsons, 2 Wis.
D. Quigg, 14 Ill. C.
W. H. Reynolds, 14 N. Y. A
J. Steele, 2 Pa. C.

* This list does not include those officers who were specially exchanged while at Charleston.

APPENDIX. 345

E. H. Smith, 2 Pa. C.
L. B. Speece, 7 Pa. V. R. Cps.
T. A. Smith, 7 Tenn. C.
M. H. Soper, 5 Ind. C.

D. Thomas, 135 O.
D. Vickers, 4 N. J.
G. G. Wanzer, 24 N. Y. C.
J. W. Young, 76 N. Y.

CAPTAINS.

J. B. Alters, 75 O.
W. N. Algbaugh, 51 Pa.
H. B. Andrews, 17 Mich.
John Aigan, 5 R. I. Art.
M. Auer, 15 N. Y. C.
C. D. Amory, A. A. Gen.
James Belger, 1 R. I. Art.
C. H. Burdick, 1 Tenn. C.
G. Bradley, 2 N. J.
C. W. Boutin, 4 Vt.
C. D. Bowen, 18 Conn.
B. Bennett, 22 N. Y. C.
N. Bostwick, 20 O.
J. F. Benson, 120 Ill.
B. C. Beebee, 13 Ind.
A. N. Benson, 1 D. C. C.
E. A. Burpee, 19 Me.
J. W. Bryant, 5 N. Y. C.
H. Biebel, 6 Conn.
J. A. Barrett, 7 Pa. R. C.
G. A. Bayard, 148 Pa.
Geo. A. Blanchard, 85 Ill.
S. Bremen, 3 Mich.
A. T. Bliss, 10 N. Y. C.
H. D. Baker, 120 Ill.
W. F. Bennett, 39 Iowa.
J. H. Brown, 17 Iowa.
S. D. Barnum, 23 U. S. C. T.
W. F. Baker, 87 Pa.
H. H. Burbank, 32 Me.
O. E. Bartlett, 31 Me.
J. T. Chalfant, 11 Pa.
C. H. Call, 29 Ill.
J. D. Clyde, 76 N. Y.
C. R. Chauncy, 34 Mass.
A. F. Cole, 59 N. Y.
J. P. Carr, 93 Ind.
H. P. Cooke, A. A. Gen.
T. B. Camp, 52 Pa.

L. S. Clark, 62 N. Y.
H. C. Chapin, 4 Vt.
F. S. Case, 2 O. C.
T. Coglin, 14 N. Y. H. Art.
J. W. Colville, 5 Mich.
L. M. Carperts, 18 Wis.
E. N. Carpenter, 6 Pa. C.
M. W. Clark, 11 Iowa C.
E. S. Daniels, 35 U. S. C. T
C. C. Dodge, 20 Mich.
O. J. Downing, 2 N. Y. C.
J. G. Derrickson, 66 N. Y
J. B. Dennis, 7 Conn.
T. F. Davenport, 75 O.
C. L. Dirlan, 12 O.
W. Dusbrow, 40 N. Y.
A. Duzenburgh, 35 N. Y.
E. B. Doane, 8 Iowa C.
W. H. Davis, 4 Md.
G. B. Donohey, 7 Pa. Res.
L. B. Davis, 93 Ind.
E C. Dicey, 1 Mich. S. S.
J. B. Dibeler, 45 Pa.
S. S. Elder, 1 U. S. Art.
B. W. Evans, 4 O. C.
M. Eagan, 15 W. Va.
N. C. Evans, 184 Pa.
W. W. Farr, 106 Pa.
E. W. Ford, 9 Minnesota.
F. W. Funk, 39 N. Y.
W. M. Fisk, 73 N. Y.
J. L. Francis, 135 Ohio.
D. Flamsburg, 4 Ind. Battery.
J. Fiedler, Eng. R. C. U. S. A.
J. P. Fall, 32 Me.
W. W. Fay, 56 Mass.
J. B. Gillespie, 120 Ill.
E. C. Gilbert, 152 N. Y.
A. W. H. Gill, 14 N. Y

APPENDIX.

E. Grant, 9 U. C.
E. H. Green, 107 Pa.
A. Grant, 19 Wis.
A. L. Goodrich, 8 N. Y. C.
J. L. Galloway, A. A. G.
J. L. Green, A. A. G. U. S. A.
C. Gutjahr, 16 Ill.
P. Grayham, 54 Pa.
H. B. Huff, 184 Pa.
W. R. Hitt, 113 Ill. C.
W. Harris, 24 Mo. C.
C. A. Hobbie, 17 Conn. C.
T. A. Heer, 28 O.
G. D. Hart, 5 Pa. C.
H. B. Hoyt, 40 N. Y. C.
D. J. Hume, 19 Mass.
R. C. Hutchison, 8 Mich.
C. W. Hastings, 12 Mass.
E. Hayes, 95 N. Y.
M C. Hobart, 7 Wis.
J. A. Hayden, 11
W L. Hodge, 120 Ill.
H A. Haines, 184 Pa.
J. B. Heltemus, 18 Ky.
S, Hymer, 115 Ill.
P. Hienrod, 105 Ohio.
F. W. Heck, 2 Md.
T. H. Hill, 2 Md.
A. J. Holmes, 37 Wis.
L. Ingledew, 7 Mich.
B. A. Jobe, 11 Pa. R. V. C.
D. Jones, 14 N. Y. Art.
S. C. Judson, 106 N. Y.
H. Jenkins, 40 Mass.
C. G. Jackson, 84 Pa.
J. D. Johnson, 10 N. J.
J. G. Kessler, 2 Ind. C.
G. E. King, 103 Ill.
P. D. Kenyon, 15 Ill. Bat.
F. Kenfield, 17 Vt.
W. S. Logan, 7 Mich.
J. S. Little, 143 Pa.
C. W. Lyttle, 145 Pa.
G. Law, 6 W. Va. C.
E. C. Latimer, 27 U. S. C. T.

W. W. McCarty, 18 Ohio.
J. W. Morton, 4 Mass. C.
J. McHugh, 69 Pa.
W. M. McFadden, 59 N. Y.
H, McCray, 115 Pa.
J. May, 15 Mass. Art.
N. H. Moore, 7 N. Y. Art.
S. F. Murray, 2 U. S. S, S.
L Marsh, 87 Pa.
A. C. Mattison, 12 N. J.
J. Metzger, 55 Pa.
Le Roy Moore, 72
S. M. Morgan, A. A. Gen.
M. McGraylis, 93 Ind.
H. P. Merrill, 4 Ky.
H. J. McDonald, 11 Conn
M. Melkorn, 135 Ohio.
J. A. Manley, 64 N. Y.
A. G. Mudgett, 11 Me.
B. J. McNitt, 1 Pa. C.
— McIntyre, 15 Wis.
L. Moore, 72 Ohio.
R. J. Millard, 2 Pa. Art.
J. H. Nutting, 27 Mass.
L. Nolan, 2 Del.
C. H. Nichols, 6 Conn.
E. E. Norton, 24 Mich.
W. H. Nash, 1 U. S. S. S.
E. Newson, 81 Ill.
A. Nuhfer, 72 Ohio.
C. Newlin. 7 Pa. C.
J. Norris, 2 Pa. Art.
C. S. Noyse, 31 Me.
H. W. Ogan, 14 Ohio.
H. V. Pemberton, 14 N. Y. A.
J. Parker, 1 N. J.
J. P. Powell, 146 N. Y.
L. B. Paine, 121 N. Y
J. T. Piggott, Jr., 8 Pa. C.
W. B. Plase, 87 U. S.
D. H. Powers, 6 Mich. C.
A. C. Paul, A. A. Gen.
G. Pettit, 120 N. Y.
D. B. Pendleton, 5 Mich. C.
D. M. Porter, 120 Ill.

APPENDIX. 347

S. C. Pieroe, 3 N. Y. C.
B. B. Porter, 10 N. Y. Art.
J. A. Paine, 2 Ind. C.
T. Ping, 17 Iowa.
J. Rourke, 1 Ill. Art.
H. Ritter, 52 N. Y.
W. J. Reynolds, 75 Ohio.
A. C. Rosencranz, 4 Ind. C.
— Reed, 107 N. Y.
R. C. Richards, 45 Pa.
W. J Reynolds, 4 R. I.
Geo. W. Reir, 107 N. Y.
C. Robinson, 31 U. S. C. T.
J. Snyder, 14 N. Y.
G. F. C. Smart, 145 Pa.
H. J. Smith, 53 Pa.
D. Schooley, 2 Pa. Art.
H. W. Strang, 30 Ill.
J. H. Smith, 16 Iowa
A. S. Skilton, 57 Ohio.
W. Shittz, 37 Ohio.
A. B. Smith, 48 Ill.
R. R. Swift, 27 Mass.
S. A. Spencer, 82 Ind.
J. R. Stevens, 40 N. Y.
E. J. Swan, 76 N. Y.
E. Schofield, 11 Pa. V. R. C.
C. B. Sutcher, 16 Ill.
E. Shurtz, 8 Iowa C.
M. L. Stansbury, 95 Ohio.
J. G. Snodgrass, 110 Ohio.
H. R. Sargent, 32 Me.
S. U. Sherman, 4 R. I.

R. T. Stewart, 138 Pa.
D. W. Scott, 23 U. S. C. T.
L. D. C. Tyler, 106 Pa.
S. C. Timpson, 95 N. Y.
H. Tilbrand, 4 N. H.
J. H. Turner, 16 Iowa.
H. G. Tibbles, 12 Ohio.
J. Thomson, 4 Ohio C.
C. L. Unthank, 11 Ky. C.
H. A. Ulffar, A. A. Gen.
J, Wnderwood, 57 Ohio.
A. Von Keiser, 30 N. Y. Bat.
Z. Vaughn, I Me. C.
A. Von Haack, 68 N. Y.
J. H. West, 11 Ky.
E. F. Wyman, ——
W. Washburn, 35 Mass.
A. R. Willis, 8 Me.
U. S. Westbrook, 135 Ohio.
B. F. Wright, 146 N. Y.
W. M. Wilson, Jr., 122 Ohio.
H. B. Wakefield, 55 Ind.
G. W. Webb, 2 Pa. Art.
J. Wilson, 57 Ohio.
R. Williams, 12 Ohio.
M. Wiley, 1 Tenn.
E. B. Whittaker, 72 Pa.
R. J. Wright, 6 Ohio,
H. H. Walpole, 122 N. Y.
M. W. Wall, 69 N. Y.
D. G. Young, 81 Ill.
E. K. Zarracher, 18 Pa. C.

LIEUTENANTS.

J. G. B. Adams, 19 Mass.
E. P. Alexander, 26 Mich.
H. M. Anderson, 3 Me.
J. F. Anderson, 2 Pa. Art.
A. L. Abbey, 8 Mich. C.
A. O. Abbott, 1 N. Y. Drag.
A. S. Appleget, 2 N. J. C.
Robert Allen, 2 N. J. Drag.
G. A. Austin, 14 Ill. Bat.
G. C. Alden, 112 Ill.

W. C. Adams, 2 Ky. C.
E. T. Affleck, 170 O. Nat. G.
E. A. Abbott, 23 O. Vet. Vol
Count S. Braiday, 2 N. J. C.
A. Bulow, 3 N. J. C.
J. H. Bryan, 184 Pa.
C. W. Baldwin, 2 N. J.
H. E. Barker, 22 N. Y. C.
C. H. Bigley, 82 N. Y.
M. Burns, 13 N. Y. C

APPENDIX.

C. A. Brown, 1 N. Y. Art.
W. R. Bospord, 1 N. Y.
J. L. Barton, 49 Pa.
W. Buchanan, 76 N. Y.
W. Blane, 43 N. Y.
J. H. Bristol, 1 Conn. C.
H. H. Bixby, 9 Me.
D. W. Burkholder, 7 Pa. V.
S. Brum, 81 Ill.
W. H. Brady, 2 Del.
J. Breon, 148 Pa.
G. N. Burnett, 4 Ind. C.
W. J. Boyd, 5 Mich. C.
S. W. Burrows, 1 N.Y. Vet. C.
M. Brickenhoff, 42 N. Y.
H. Buckley, 4 N. H. Vol.
A. T. Barnes, Ill. Vet. Batt.
J. L. Beasley, 81 Ill.
A. Barringer, 44 N. Y.
F. P. Bishop, 4 Tenn. C.
C. T. Bowen, 4 R. I.
Wm. Bateman, 9 Mich. C.
Wm. Baird, 23 U. S. C. T.
J. N. Biller, 2 Pa. Art.
F. S. Bowley, 30 U. S. C. T.
C. Boettger, 2 Md.
W. A. Barnard, 20 Mich.
Wm. Blasse, 43 N. Y.
C. O. Brown, 81 Me.
R. K. Beecham, 23 U. S. C. T.
A. M. Briscol, Cole's Md. C.
H. M. Bearce, 32 Me.
A. J. Braidy, 54 Pa.
C. A. Bell, A. D. C.
R. Burton, 9 N. Y. Art.
H. E. Beebee, 22 N. Y. C.
V. L. Coffin, 31 Me.
L. A. Campbell, 152 N. Y.
C. W. Carr, 4 Vt.
J. Cunningham, 7 Pa. R. C.
C. Coslett, 115 Pa.
R. Cooper, 7 N. J.
C. H. Crawford, 183 Pa.
S. O. Cromack, 77 N. Y.
H. Correll, 2 Vt.

C. H. Cutter, 95 Ill
G. W. Creacy, 35 Mass.
R. H. Chute, 59 Mass.
H. M. Cross, 59 Mass.
H. A. Chapin, 95 N. Y.
W. Chahill, 76 N. Y.
J. L. Casler, 76 N. Y.
H. Chisman, 7 Ind.
H. Cribben, 140 N. Y.
G. M. Curtis, 140 N. Y.
J. S. Calwell, 16 Ill. C.
S. Crossley, 118 Pa.
L. B. Carlisle, 145 Pa.
J. P. Codington, 8 Iowa C.
W. H. Curtis, 19 Mass.
J. W. Clark, 59 N. Y.
J. H. Clark, 1 Mass. Art.
D. L. Case, Jr., 102 N. Y.
J. D. Cope, 116 Pa.
J. W. Core, 6 W. Va. C.
W. J. Colter, 15 Mass.
J. Casey, 45 N. Y.
W. H. Carter, 5 Pa. R. C.
J. L. Chittenden, 5 Ind. C.
W. H. Canney, 69 N. Y.
W. F. Campbell, 51 Pa.
J. F. Cameron, 5 Pa. C.
M. Clegg, 5 Ind. C.
H. R. Chase, 1 Vt. H. Art.
W. H. Conover, 22 N. Y. C.
D. F. Califf, 2 W. S. S. S
D. B. Chubbuck, 19 Mass.
M. Cunningham, 42 N. Y.
A. M. Charters, 17 Iowa.
W. A. Copeland, 10 Mich.
T. Clemons, 13 Ill.
W. C. Cook, 9 Mich. C.
C. P. Cramer, 21 N. Y. C.
Geo. Corum, 2 Ky. C.
M. B. Case, 23 U. S. C. T.
D. J. Cline, 75 O. V. M. I.
C. G. Conn, 1 M. S. S.
M. Cunningham, 1 Vt. H. A.
C. D. Copeland, 58 Pa.
C. P. Cashell, 12 Pa. C.

APPENDIX. 349

J. R. Charnel, 1 Ill. Art.
W. S. Damrell, 13 Mass.
W. G. Davis, 27 Mass.
S. V. Dean, 145 Pa.
J. S. Drennan, 1 Vt. Art.
J. Dunn, 64 N. Y.
A. J. Dunning, 7 N. Y. Art.
J. Donovan, 2 N. J.
E. B. Dyre, 1 Conn. C.
W. C. Dorris, 111 Ill.
H. G. Dodge, 2 Pa. C.
C. Downs, 33 N. J.
J. Duven, 5 N. H.
W. H. Dorfee, 5 R. I.
G. Dorbine, 66 N. Y.
W. H. Dieffenbach, 7 Pa. Res.
R. De Lay, 3 Iowa C.
O. W. Demmick, 11 N. H.
L. Dick, 72 O.
E. Dickerson, 44 Wis.
D. Driscoll, 24 Mo.
H. G. Dorr, 4 Mass. C.
J. M. Drake, 9 N. J.
H. A. Downing, 31 U. S. C. T.
J. W. Davison, 95 O.
G. H. Drew, 9 N. H.
Chas. Everrett, 70 Ohio.
F. R. Eastman, 2 Pa. C.
J. L. F. Elkin, 1 N. J.
T. E. Evans, 52 Pa.
J. W. Eyestone, 13 Ind.
T. K. Eckings, 3 N. J.
John Eagan, 1 U. S. A.
John Elder, 8 Ind.
J. Fairbanks, 72 Ohio.
G. E. Finney, 19 Ind.
J. M. Ferris, 3 Mich.
E. M. Faye, 42 N. Y.
J. Furgeson, 1 N. J.
D. Flannery, 4 N. J.
H. M. Fowler, 15 N. J.
G. W. Flager, 11 Pa. R. C.
C. A. Fagan, 11 Pa. R. C.
H. French, 3 Vt.
L. W. Fisher, 4 Vt.

S. Fatzer, 108 N. Y.
E. Fontaine, 7 Pa. R. C.
D. Forney, 30 O.
S. Fisher, 93 Ind.
D. S. Finney, 14 and 15 Ill. V.
L. Pitzpatrick, 146 N. Y.
L. D. C. Fales, ——
H. C. Foster, 23 Ind.
John Foley, 59 Mass.
Louis Faass, 14 N. Y. Art.
R. J. Frost, 9 Mich. C.
G. J. George, 40 Ill.
T. M. Gunn, 21 Ky.
J. Gottshell, 55 Pa.
J. M. Godown, 12 Ind.
H. D. Grant, 117 N. Y.
J. A. Goodwin, 1 Mass. C.
C. V. Granger, 88 N. Y.
C. O. Gordon, 1 Me. C.
J. W. Goss, 1 Mass. Art.
H. M. Gordon, 143 Pa.
J. Gallagher, 4 Ohio Vet.
E. A. Green, 81 Ill.
T. Griffen, 55 U. S. C. T.
M. L. Godley, 17 Iowa.
Philip Grey, 72 Pa.
A. M. Hall, 9 Minn.
E. R. Hart, 1 Vt. Art
J. F. Hodge, 55 Pa.
R. F. Hall, 75 Ohio.
J. T. Haight, 8 Iowa C.
G. W. Hill, 7 Mich. C.
E. J. Hazel, 6 Pa. C.
R. Herbert, 50 Pa.
S. H. Horton, 101 Pa.
W. B. Hurd, 17 Mich. C.
E. Holden, 1 Vt. C.
S. P. Hedges, 112 N. Y. C.
H. C. Hinds, 102 N. Y.
J. Hopper, 2 N. Y. C.
C. O. Hunt, 5 Me. Bat.
W. R. Hulland, 5 Md. C.
G. W. Hull, 135 Ohio.
D. W. Hazelton, 22 N. Y. C.
C. P. Holaham, 19 Pa. C.

350   APPENDIX.

H. N. Hamilton, 59 N. Y.
E. S. Huntington, 11 U. S.
W. H. Hoyt, 16 Iowa.
R. M. Hughes, 14 Ill. C.
J. Hewitt, 105 Pa.
J. Heston, 4 N. J.
J. Heffelfinger, 7 Pa. R. V.
J. L. Harvey, 2 Pa. Art.
H. V. Hadley, 7 Ind.
M. V. B. Hallett, 2 Pa. C.
A. J. Henry, 120 Ill.
V. G. Hoalladay, 2 Ind. C.
D. Havens, 85 Ill.
C. A. Hays, 11 Pa.
J. L. Hastings, 7 Pa. R. V. C.
J. W. Harris, 2 Ind. C.
F. Herzbery, 66 N. Y.
J. T. Haight, 8 Iowa C.
E. H. Higley, 1 Vt. C.
W. H. Hendryks, 11 Mich. B.
J. Huston, 95 Ohio.
R. Henderson, 1 Mass. Art.
A. N. Hackett, 110 O.
S. P. Hand, 43 U. S. C. T.
T. B. Hurst, 7 Pa. Res. V. C.
Geo. Hopf, 2 Md.
O. M. Hill, 1 Mo. Art.
J. B. Hogue, 4 Pa. C.
L. E. Haywood, 58 Mass.
A. B. Isham, 7 Mich. C.
H. A. Johnson, 3 Me.
C. K. Johnson, 1 Me. C.
G. W. Jenkins, 9 W. Va.
J. C. Justus, 2 Pa. R. V. C.
S. E. Jones, 7 N. Y. Art.
J. W. Johnson, 1 Mass. Art.
Alfred Jones, 50 Pa. Vet.
J. Jacks, 15 W. Va.
P. Krohn, 5 N. Y. C.
E. Kendrick, 10 N. J.
S. C. Kerr, 126 Ohio.
H. T. Kendall, 50 Pa.
A. Kelly, 126 Ohio.
J. Keen, 7 Pa. V. R. C.
J D. Kennuly, 8 Ohio C.

J. F. Kempton, 75 Ohio.
J. H. Kidd, 1 Md. Art.
R. H. Kendrick, 25 Wis.
G. C. Kenyon, 17 Ill.
G. C. Kidder, 113 Pa.
G. Knox, 109 Pa.
J. M. Kelly, 4 Tenn.
F. H. Kempton, 58 Mass. Art.
J. R. Kelly, 1 Pa. C.
J. C. Knox, 4 Ind. C.
Abe King, 12 Ohio.
J. Kepheart, 13 Ohio.
J. Kellow, 2 Pa. Art.
G. L. Kibby, 4 R. I.
C. E. Lewis, 1 N. Y. Drag.
J. B. Laycock, 7 Pa. R. V. C.
H. H. Lyman, 147 N. Y.
W. H. Larrabee, 7 Me.
A. Lee, 152 N. Y.
J. L. Lynn, 145 Pa.
E. De C. Loud, 2 Pa. Art.
M. S. Ludwig, 53 Pa.
D. W. Lowry, 2 Pa. Art.
J. Lyman, 27 Mass.
J. O. Laird, 35 U. S.
M. Laird, 16 Iowa.
J. C. Luther, Pa. V. R. C.
M. W. Lemon, 14 N. Y. Art.
L. M. Lane, 9 Minn.
T. D. Lamson, 3 Ind. C. [Q. M.
A. Limbard, McLaughlin's S.
G. H. Lawrence, 2 N. Y. M. R.
C. H. Lang, 59 Mass.
J. Monaghan, 62 Pa.
J. C. McIntosh, 145 Pa.
F. W. Mather, 7 N. Y. Art.
P. B. Mockrie, 7 N. Y. Art.
E. T. McCutcheon, 64 N. Y.
E. J. McWain, 1 N. Y. Art.
J. McKage, 184 Pa.
S. F. Muffley, 184 Pa.
H. F. Mangus, 53 Pa.
J. McLaughlin, 53 Pa.
W. A. McGinnes, 19 Mass.
A. D. Mathews, 1 Vt. Art.

APPENDIX.

A. Morse, 1 Vt. Art.
J. H. Morris, 4 Ky.
W. H. Myers, 76 N. Y.
J. McGeehan, 146 N. Y.
H. W. Mitchell, 14 N. Y.
J. C. McCain, 9 Minn.
T. McGuire, 7 Ill.
J. W. Miller, 14 Ill. C.
J. Murphy, 69 N. Y.
J. Mallison, 94 N. Y.
J. A. Mullegan, 4 Mass. C.
W. F. Mathews, 1 Md.
N. J. Menier, 93 Ind.
H. Miller, 17 Mich.
P. W. McMannus, 27 Mass.
E. McMahon, 72 Ohio.
G. C. Morton, 4 Pa. C.
E. Mather, 1 Vt. C.
C. McDonald, 2 Ill. Art.
G. W. Mayer, 37 Ind.
J. McCormick, 21 N. Y. C.
A. J. Marshland, 2 Pa. Art.
W. H. Mix, 19 U. S. C. T.
T. J. Munger, 37 Wis.
A. McNure, 73 Pa.
H. G. Mitchell, 32 Me.
J. D. Marshall, 57 O.
McLane, 9 Minn.
C. Niedenhoffen, 9 Minn.
A. Nelson, 66 N. Y.
J. B. Meedham, 4 Vt.
C. L. Noggle, 2 U. S.
J. Norwood, 76 N. Y.
O. H. Nealy, 11 U. S.
W. McM. Nettervill, 12 U. S.
W. Neher, 7 Pa. R. V. C.
A. Neal, 5 Ind. C.
D. M. Niswander, 2 Pa. Art.
H. J. Nyman, 19 Mich.
W. R. Nulland, 5 Ind. C.
R. V. Outcolt, 135 O.
J. O. Harre, 7 N. Y. Art.
F. Osborne, 19 Mass.
D. Oliphant, 35 N. J.
E. O. Shea, 13 Pa. C.

R. O'Connell, 55 Pa.
J. Ogden, 1 Wis. C.
G. C. Olden, 112 Ill.
A. C. Pickenpaugh, 6 W. Va.
H. Picquet, 32 Ill.
J. T. Parker, 13 Iowa.
A. Phinney, 90 Ill.
W. M. Provine, 84 Ill.
T. Purcell, 16 Iowa.
W. H. Powell, 2 Ill. L. Art.
G. M. Parker, 45 Ill.
J. S. Purveance, 130 Ind.
D. H. Piffard, 14 N. Y.
C. A. Price, 5 Mich.
E. B. Parker, 1 Vt. Art.
W. H. Patridge, 67 N. Y.
H. H. Pierce, 7 Conn.
G. W. Pitt, 85 N. Y. Vet.
L. S. Peake, 85 N. Y. Vet.
E. C. Pierson, 85 N. Y. Vet.
D. Pentzell, 4 N. Y. C.
J. G. Peetrey, 95 Ohio.
M. P. Pierson, 100 N. Y.
A. L. Preston, 8 Mich. C.
G. Peters, 9 N. J.
J. H. Pitt, 118 N. Y.
James Post, 149 ——.
W. D. Peck, 2 N J. C.
G. W. Paterson, 135 Ohio.
J. C. Price, 75 Ohio.
Z. Perrin, 72 Ohio.
S. H. Platt, 34 Mass.
L. G. Porter, 81 Ill.
J. H. Palmer, 12 Ohio.
W. A. Pope, 18 Wis.
D. B. Pyne, 8 Mo.
Worthington Pierce, 17 Vt
W. B. Phillips, 2 Pa. Art.
C. O. Poindexter, 31 Me.
A. P. Pierson, 9 Mich. C.
Chas. A. Price, 3 Mich.
M. Rees, 72 Ohio.
W. B. Rose, 73 Ill.
J. M. Ruger, 57 Pa.
L. S. Richards, 1 Vt. Art

J. R. Borsnels, 145 Pa.
G. Ricneckar, 5 Pa. C.
O. Rahu, 184 Pa.
G. A. Rowley, 2 U. S.
B. E. Robinson, 95 O.
W. E. Roach, 49 N. Y.
H. W. Raymond, 8 N. Y. Art.
J. E. Rose, 120 Ill.
E. R. Roberts, 7 Ill.
J. H. Reed, 120 Ill.
J. M. Richards, 1 W. Va.
H. Rothe, 15 N. Y. Art.
E. K. Ramsey, 1 N. J.
L. H. Riley, 7 Pa. R. V. C.
C. H. Ross, 13 Ind.
A. Ring, 12 Ohio.
T. Rathbone, 153 Ohio.
C. L. Rugg, 6 Ind. C.
J. S. Rice, 13 Ind.
J. Reade, 57 Mass.
A. J. Raynor, 19 U. S. C. T.
L. Rainer, 2 N. J. C.
J. S. Robeson, 7 Tenn. C.
W. L. Riley, 21 N. Y. C.
W. H. Randall, 1 Mich. S. S.
W. B. Sturgeon, 107 Pa.
M. H. Stover, 184 Pa.
A. A. Sweetland, 2 Pa. C.
E. B. Smith, 1 Vt. Art.
C. Schurr, 7 N. Y. Art.
W. H. Shafer, 5 Pa. C.
M. G. Sargeant, 1 Vt. Art.
C. H. Stallman, 87 Pa. Art.
S. S. Smythe, 1 Ill. Art.
Geo. Scott, 10 Ind.
E. Swift, 74 Ill.
J. L. Skinner, 27 Mass.
F. Stevens, 190 Pa.
C. Stuart, 24 N. Y.
M. Shanan, 140 N. Y.
M. S. Smith, 16 Me.
E. Snowwhite, 7 Pa. V. R. C.
W. H. S. Sweet, 146 N. Y
J. R. Sitler, 2 Pa. C.
A. L. Shannon, 3 Ind. C.

A. M. Smith, 1 Tenn. C.
J. C. Smith, 24 Ind. Bat.
J. B. Smith, 5 W. Va. C.
W. Sandon, 1 Wis. C.
J. P. Smith, 49 Pa.
J. G. Stevens, 52 Pa.
C. T. Swope, 4 Ky.
A. S. Stewart, 4 Ky.
E. P. Strickland, 114 Ill.
P. Smith, 4 Tenn. C.
J. W. Stanton, 5 Ind. C.
W. H. St. John, 5 Ind. C.
F. E. Scripture, R. Q. M.
A. B. Simmons, 5 Ind. C.
H. P. Starr, 22 N. Y. C.
B. Spring, 75 Ohio.
A. C. Stover, 95 O.
C. P. Stone, 1 Vt. C.
J. Stebbins, 77 N. Y.
C. S. Schwartz, 2 N. J. C.
J. Sailor, 13 Pa. C.
H. C. Smyser, 2 Md.
B. R. Stewart, 2 N. Y. C.
M. W. Striblings, 61 Ohio.
J. Smith, 5 Pa. C. [Ohio C.
J. O. Stout, McLaughlin's S.
M. N. Shepstrong, 60 Ohio.
J. W. Stanton, 5 Ind. C.
J. P. Sheehan, 31 Me.
J. F. Shull, 28 U. S. C. T.
S. B. Smith, 30 U. S. C. T.
B. F. Stauber, 20 Pa. C.
H. Schulter, 43 N. Y.
L. D. Seely, 45 Pa.
Frank Stevens, 12 Pa. V.R. C.
A. F. Septon, 8 Iowa C.
T. D. Scofield, 27 Mich.
C. B. Sanders, 30 U. S. C. T.
P. A. Simondson, 23 U. S.C.T.
N. W. Shaefer, 24 Ind. C.
H. S. Tainter, 82 N. Y.
D. Tanner, 118 Ill.
H. V. Tompkins, 59 N. Y.
B. W. Trout, 106 Pa.
J. S. Tompson, 10 Vt.

APPENDIX. 353

L. E. Tyler, 1 Conn. C.
A. Timm, 16 Iowa.
O. Todd, 18 Wis.
A. W. Tiffany, 9 Minn.
J. Taylor, 2 Pa. V. R. C.
D. W. Tower, 17 Iowa.
F. Tomson, 17 Iowa.
A. F. Tipton, 8 Iowa C.
David Turmer, 118 Ill.
C. Tobel, 15 N. Y. Art.
J. P. F. Toby, 31 Me.
S. H. Tinker, 93 Ind.
D. D. Von Valack, 12 U. S.
D. Van Doren, 72 Ohio.
C. Van Rensalaer, 148 N. Y.
W. C. Van Alin, 45 Pa.
A. Von Bulow, 3 N. J. C.
O. W. West, 1 N. Y. Drag.
J. B. Warner, 8 Mich. C.
G. Williams, 8 Mich. C.
J. Winters, 72 Ohio.
J. Warner, 33 N. J.
J. F. Wheeler, 149 N. Y.
F. Waidmann, 16 Iowa.
J. Walker, 8 Tenn.
T. A. Weesner, 14 and 15 Ill.
G. J. West, 6 Conn.
D. H. Wing, 14 N. Y. Art.

C. W. Wilcox, 9 N. H.
J. C. Watson, 126 Ohio.
F. M. Woodruff, 76 N. Y.
Geo. Weddle, 144 Ohio.
C. W. Woodrow, 19 Iowa.
H. H. Willis, 40 N. Y.
J. Winship, 88 Ill.
R. Wilson, 113 Ill.
B. F. Whitten, 9 Me.
J. W. Warren, 1 Wis. C.
W. Williams, 8 Mich. C.
T. H. Ward, 59 U. S. C. T.
J. Wheaton, 59 U. S. C. T.
B. W. Whittemore, 5 N. Y. C.
H. A. Wentworth, 14 N. Y. A.
W. H. Walker, 4 Ohio.
E. S. Wilson, 1 Mass. C.
D. H. Warren, A. Surg. 8 I. C.
R. P. Wilson, 5 U. S. C.
E. C. Taw, 67 N. Y.
J. H. York, 63 Ind.
W. J. Young, 111 Ill.
A. Young, 4 Pa. C.
T. P. Young, 4 Ky.
Aaron Zeigler, 7 Pa. V. R. C.
A. Zimm, 15 Iowa.
C. Zobel, 15 N. Y. A.

THE END.